THE ULTIMATE GUIDE TO MODERN ETIQUETTE

MASTERING MANNERS AND SOCIAL SKILLS FOR ANY SITUATION

REBECCA FERGUSON

❀ Created with Vellum

FOREWORD

As I sit down to introduce this book, I'm reminded of the countless interactions I've had over the years—both in my personal life and throughout my career as a relationship coach. These experiences have shaped my understanding of etiquette as something far deeper than a set of rigid rules. Rather, etiquette is the art of showing care and respect in every encounter, a practice that weaves the fabric of our social lives together, whether we're engaging with loved ones or strangers, in familiar surroundings or across cultures.

Over the past two decades, I've had the privilege of working with individuals from all walks of life. My journey has taken me from the joy of celebrating milestones with clients to guiding them through some of their most challenging moments. Along the way, I've witnessed how the principles of good manners—thoughtfulness, empathy, and respect—can transform relationships and create a more harmonious world.

In writing this book, I wanted to bring a modern perspective to the age-old concept of etiquette. Our world is more diverse and interconnected than ever before, and it's essential that our understanding of social graces evolves to reflect this reality. This book is not just about how to navigate traditional social settings; it's also about how to engage meaningfully with the wide array of communities that make up our world today. Whether you're interacting with people from different cultural backgrounds, respecting gender diversity, or simply learning to be more mindful of others' experiences, this book aims to equip you with the tools to do so with grace and confidence.

I've lived overseas for five years, traveled to more than 20 countries, and had the honor of meeting people from an incredible diversity of backgrounds. These experiences have taught me that the heart of etiquette lies in inclusivity. It's about recognizing and honoring the richness of the human experience, in all its varied forms. This book seeks to be a guide for everyone—for those who wish to navigate life's social complexities with kindness and for those who wish to deepen their understanding of how to interact with the world around them in a way that fosters connection and respect.

You'll find that this book covers a wide range of topics, from dining and travel etiquette to the more nuanced areas of gender and cultural sensitivity. Each chapter is designed to offer practical advice while also encouraging reflection on how we can all contribute to a more inclusive and understanding society.

As you embark on this journey through the pages of this book, my hope is that you'll come away not only with a better grasp of social etiquette but also with a renewed commitment to treating others with the dignity and respect they deserve. In today's fast-paced and often divided world, these principles are more important than ever.

Thank you for allowing me to share these insights with you. I'm excited to join you on this journey toward more thoughtful, inclusive, and gracious living.

Rebecca Ferguson

Relationship Coach, Author, and Advocate for Inclusive Etiquette

INTRODUCTION

The Importance of Etiquette in Today's World

In our rapidly evolving society, where technology bridges distances and brings diverse cultures closer together, the importance of etiquette remains steadfast. Etiquette, often defined as the customary code of polite behavior in society or among members of a particular profession or group, serves as a framework for navigating social interactions with grace and respect. It is more than just a set of rules; it is a reflection of our consideration for others and our awareness of the impact our actions have on those around us.

As a relationship coach with over 20 years of experience, I've seen how understanding and practicing good etiquette can transform relationships. I've worked with individuals struggling to connect with others, whether in personal or professional settings, and have guided them toward more positive, respectful interactions. Through these experiences, I've learned that etiquette is not about following a strict set of rules, but about cultivating an attitude of empathy and respect that can profoundly impact our relationships and our lives.

Why Etiquette Matters in the Modern Age

Etiquette matters because it fosters harmony in our interactions, both personal and professional. As we move through our daily lives, we encounter a wide range of social situations, each with its own expectations and norms. Whether it's a formal business meeting, a casual dinner with friends, or an online conversation, knowing how to conduct ourselves appropriately ensures that these interactions are smooth, respectful, and productive. In the modern age, where the pace of life is faster and the boundaries between personal and professional spaces are often blurred, etiquette provides the structure we need to maintain positive relationships and avoid misunderstandings.

Over the years, I've observed how even small acts of courtesy—such as a well-timed thank you or a thoughtful gesture—can make a significant difference in the way we are perceived and how we connect with others. In a world where we often communicate more through screens than face-to-face, these small but meaningful actions can bridge gaps, build trust, and create a sense of connection that is increasingly rare.

The Role of Manners and Social Skills in Personal and Professional Success

Manners and social skills are the building blocks of successful interactions. In personal relationships, they help us connect with others on a deeper level, showing that we value and respect their presence in our lives. In professional settings, good manners can set us apart, creating a positive impression that can lead to new opportunities and collaborations. Social skills, such as effective communication, active listening, and empathy, are essential in both realms, helping us navigate complex situations with confidence and ease. By mastering these skills, we can build stronger, more meaningful connections with those around us, enhancing our personal and professional lives.

Throughout my career, I've seen how mastering these skills can open doors that might otherwise remain closed. Clients who once struggled with social anxiety or professional stagnation have found that improving their manners and social skills not only enhances their relationships but also boosts their confidence and overall well-being. Whether it's learning to listen more actively, express gratitude more freely, or manage conflicts with grace, these skills are integral to leading a successful and fulfilling life.

How This Book Will Help You Navigate Social Situations with Confidence

"The Ultimate Guide to Modern Etiquette: Mastering Manners and Social Skills for Every Situation" is designed to be your comprehensive resource for understanding and applying the principles of etiquette in today's world. Whether you are navigating the nuances of workplace interactions, seeking to improve your dating etiquette, or simply looking to enhance your everyday social skills, this book offers practical advice and insights tailored to the needs of the modern individual. Each chapter delves into specific areas of etiquette, providing clear guidelines and real-world examples to help you feel confident in any social situation. By the end of this book, you will have the tools you need to present yourself with poise and professionalism, no matter the context.

My own journey with etiquette has been shaped by both personal and professional experiences. I've seen firsthand how understanding the unwritten rules of social interaction can change lives—how it can turn a tense meeting into a productive dialogue, or transform an awkward first date into the start of something special. Through this book, I hope to share the lessons I've learned, helping you to navigate the complexities of social interactions with the same ease and confidence that I've seen in the most successful individuals.

A Brief History of Etiquette

Etiquette has been an integral part of human society for centuries, evolving alongside our cultural, social, and technological advancements. To fully appreciate the role of etiquette in our lives today, it is important to understand its origins and how it has transformed over time.

What Is Etiquette?

At its core, etiquette is the set of conventional rules that govern social behavior within a particular group or society. These rules are not arbitrary; they are rooted in the shared values and norms of a community, designed to promote respect, consideration, and smooth interaction among its members. Etiquette can be as formal as the protocols followed in diplomatic settings or as simple as the everyday courtesies we extend to others in our daily lives. Regardless of the context, etiquette helps us navigate the complexities of social interactions, ensuring that we can communicate effectively, avoid offense, and build positive relationships.

In my work, I often remind clients that etiquette is not about perfection, but about intention. It's about striving to make others feel valued and respected, whether through a warm smile, a sincere apology, or a well-timed gesture of kindness. These small acts, guided by an understanding of etiquette, are what build the trust and connection that underpin all successful relationships.

The Evolution of Etiquette Through the Ages

The concept of etiquette has been present in human societies for millennia, with its formalization beginning in the courts of Renaissance Europe. During this time, elaborate rules of behavior were developed to maintain order and decorum in royal courts. These rules were later codified in etiquette manuals, which became essential guides for the aristocracy. As society progressed, these practices filtered down to the middle and lower classes, evolving into the more accessible social norms we recognize today. The Victorian era, in particular, saw a heightened emphasis on etiquette, with rigid expectations governing every aspect of social life. However, as the world modernized, so too did the concept of etiquette, adapting to the changing social structures and the democratization of society.

In today's world, I've noticed that while the formalities of the past have relaxed, the core principles of etiquette—respect, consideration, and empathy—remain as relevant as ever. Whether we're engaging in a business negotiation or simply sharing a meal with friends, these principles guide our interactions and help us navigate the increasingly complex social landscapes we encounter.

The Distinction Between Traditional and Modern Etiquette

While traditional etiquette often emphasized rigid rules and strict adherence to social hierarchies, modern etiquette is more flexible and inclusive. Today's etiquette places a greater emphasis on empathy, cultural sensitivity, and respect for diversity. It is less about following a prescribed set of rules and more about understanding the principles that underlie courteous behavior. This shift reflects the changing dynamics of our society, where equality, inclusivity, and mutual respect are increasingly valued. Modern etiquette also adapts to new social contexts, such as the digital realm, where the rules of engagement are still evolving.

Over the years, I've guided many clients through the challenges of adapting to these modern expectations. Whether they're navigating the nuances of online communication, managing cross-cultural interactions, or simply trying to be more considerate in their daily lives, the principles of modern etiquette provide the foundation they need to succeed. It's about being adaptable, empathetic, and always mindful of the impact our actions have on others.

Understanding Cultural Differences in Manners

In a globalized world, where interactions across cultures are commonplace, understanding and respecting cultural differences in manners is essential. What is considered polite in one culture may be perceived differently in another. For example, the custom of exchanging business cards in Japan involves a formal presentation with both hands, reflecting respect and attentiveness, whereas in Western cultures, a simple exchange with one hand is common. Recognizing these differences and adapting our behavior accordingly demonstrates cultural awareness and respect, qualities that are increasingly important in today's interconnected world.

Through this book, you will explore these cultural nuances and learn how to apply the principles of modern etiquette across various social contexts. By combining the timeless values of respect and consideration with the practical demands of contemporary life, "The Ultimate Guide to Modern Etiquette" aims to equip you with the skills and confidence to navigate any situation with ease and grace.

As you journey through the chapters of this book, you will gain a deeper understanding of the role that etiquette plays in our daily lives. From the boardroom to the dining table, from formal events to casual gatherings, etiquette is the key to building and maintaining relationships that are respectful, positive, and fulfilling. Whether you are seeking to refine your social skills or simply looking to understand the unwritten rules of modern society, this guide will serve as your trusted companion, helping you to master the art of etiquette in every situation.

My hope is that, through this book, you will not only learn the practical aspects of etiquette but also embrace the deeper principles of respect, empathy, and kindness that truly make etiquette a powerful tool for personal and professional success. These principles have guided me throughout my career and my personal life, helping me to build meaningful connections and navigate even the most challenging social situations with confidence and grace. I invite you to join me on this journey, as we explore together the enduring importance of etiquette in our modern world.

ONE

THE FOUNDATIONS OF MODERN ETIQUETTE

ETIQUETTE IS OFTEN ASSOCIATED with a set of rules, but at its heart, it's about principles that guide our interactions with others. These principles—respect, kindness, and consideration—form the foundation of good manners and help us navigate the complexities of modern social life. In this chapter, we will delve into these core principles, explore the role of social norms, and discuss essential etiquette skills. I'll also share practical tips and exercises to help you apply these concepts in your daily life, drawing from my experiences as a relationship coach where I've seen firsthand the transformative power of good manners.

The Core Principles of Good Manners

Respect, Kindness, and Consideration for Others

Respect is the cornerstone of all good manners. It's about recognizing the inherent worth of every individual and treating them with dignity, regardless of differences. Respect manifests in our behavior—how we speak, listen, and respond to others. Kindness, closely related to respect, is the active expression of goodwill. It's about being thoughtful and supportive, going out of your way to make others feel valued. Consideration involves being mindful of how our actions affect others, ensuring that our behavior promotes harmony and avoids causing discomfort or harm.

In my two decades as a relationship coach, I've seen how these simple yet profound principles can change the course of a conversation, a relationship, and even a person's life. For instance, I've worked with clients who struggled with expressing kindness or respecting boundaries, and I've watched them transform their interactions by consciously applying these principles. It's not about being perfect; it's about striving to make others feel respected and valued in every encounter.

The Importance of Empathy in Social Interactions

Empathy is the ability to understand and share another person's feelings. It's crucial in social interactions because it fosters deeper connections and smoother communication. When you approach interactions with empathy, you're more likely to listen effectively, resolve conflicts peacefully, and build stronger relationships. Empathy also helps you navigate difficult situations with sensitivity, ensuring that your actions align with the needs and feelings of others.

I've witnessed how empathy can bridge gaps between people, whether in personal relationships or professional settings. I remember a client who struggled with workplace conflicts, often finding herself at odds with colleagues. By learning to approach these situations with empathy, she was able to see things from others' perspectives, which not only improved her relationships but also her overall job satisfaction. Empathy isn't just a nice-to-have skill; it's a powerful tool for creating harmony and understanding in our interactions.

How to Apply These Principles in Everyday Life

Applying respect, kindness, and empathy in everyday life requires mindfulness and intention. Here are some practical ways to integrate these principles into your daily interactions:

- **Listen actively:** Focus fully on the person speaking, avoid interrupting, and show that you're engaged. This simple act can make the other person feel heard and valued, laying the foundation for a positive interaction.
- **Use polite language:** Simple phrases like "please," "thank you," and "excuse me" demonstrate respect and consideration. These words may seem small, but they carry significant weight in how they make others feel.
- **Be punctual:** Respect others' time by being on time for appointments and meetings. Punctuality shows that you value the other person's time as much as your own.
- **Show appreciation:** Acknowledge others' efforts with sincere thanks, whether through words or small gestures. A thank-you note or a simple acknowledgment can go a long way in strengthening relationships.
- **Respect personal space:** Be aware of physical boundaries and avoid behaviors that might make others uncomfortable. Understanding and respecting these boundaries is a key aspect of showing consideration for others.

Understanding Social Norms

The Role of Social Norms in Guiding Behavior

Social norms are the unwritten rules that govern behavior within a society. They help us understand what is considered acceptable, appropriate, or respectful in different situations. These norms vary across cultures and contexts, providing a framework for behavior that promotes social harmony.

In my work, I've seen how social norms can both guide and sometimes constrain behavior. For example, a client once felt pressured to conform to certain social norms at work that didn't align with her values. Through our sessions, she learned how to navigate these expectations while staying true to herself, showing that understanding norms is the first step in deciding how to respond to them.

Adapting to Different Social Contexts and Settings

Understanding and adapting to social norms is essential for navigating different social contexts. For instance, what's appropriate in a formal business meeting may differ significantly from a casual gathering with friends. Being observant and attuned to the behavior of those around you will help you adjust your actions to suit the setting.

I often encourage my clients to observe before acting in unfamiliar social settings. Whether they're at a networking event or a new social group, taking the time to understand the dynamics at play can prevent missteps and help them integrate more smoothly. This adaptability is a skill that can be honed over time, leading to more confident and appropriate social interactions.

Recognizing When to Follow or Challenge Traditional Norms

Not all social norms are beneficial or inclusive. Some traditional norms may be outdated or discriminatory, requiring us to challenge them thoughtfully. For example, outdated gender norms or hierarchical structures may no longer be relevant. Challenging such norms with respect and empathy can help create a more inclusive and equitable environment.

I've seen firsthand how challenging traditional norms can lead to positive change. One client, frustrated by the rigid gender roles in her workplace, took a stand by advocating for more inclusive policies. Her efforts not only improved her own work environment but also paved the way for others to feel more comfortable expressing their true selves. Challenging norms isn't always easy, but it can be incredibly rewarding when done thoughtfully and respectfully.

Basic Etiquette Skills

The Art of Introductions: How to Introduce Yourself and Others

Introductions set the tone for any interaction. Here's how to make a positive impression:

- **Introducing Yourself:** Start with a friendly greeting and your name, like "Hello, I'm Jane Doe. It's nice to meet you." Make eye contact, smile, and offer a firm handshake if appropriate. These simple actions convey confidence and respect.
- **Introducing Others:** Introduce the person of higher rank or importance first. For example, "Mr. Smith, I'd like you to meet my colleague, Sarah Johnson." Providing context helps both parties understand the relevance of the introduction, making the interaction smoother and more meaningful.

Over the years, I've seen how mastering the art of introductions can significantly impact relationships. A warm, well-executed introduction can set the stage for a positive interaction, while a poorly handled one can create awkwardness or misunderstandings. Practicing these skills until they become second nature can make all the difference in your social and professional life.

The Essentials of Polite Conversation

Polite conversation is the foundation of social interaction. Here's how to ensure your conversations are respectful and engaging:

- **Listen more than you speak:** Show interest by listening attentively and asking thoughtful questions. This not only makes the other person feel valued but also enriches the conversation.
- **Avoid controversial topics:** Steer clear of subjects like politics or religion in casual settings, focusing instead on neutral topics like hobbies or current events. This helps maintain a positive and inclusive atmosphere.
- **Be mindful of tone and language:** Use a friendly, respectful tone, and avoid jargon or overly casual language in formal settings. The way you speak can significantly influence how your message is received.
- **Know when to end a conversation:** Recognize social cues that indicate it's time to wrap up and do so politely. Ending a

conversation graciously leaves a positive impression and opens the door for future interactions.

I've worked with many individuals who struggled with conversation skills, often feeling nervous or unsure of what to say. Through practice and reflection, they've learned to navigate conversations with ease, making connections that were once out of reach. The ability to engage in polite, thoughtful conversation is a skill that will serve you well in every aspect of your life.

Common Courtesies: Please, Thank You, Excuse Me

These simple phrases are powerful tools for showing respect and consideration:

- **Please:** Softens requests, showing that you're not taking the other person's help for granted. It's a small word with a big impact, setting the tone for a respectful interaction.
- **Thank You:** Expresses gratitude for someone's efforts, no matter how small. A sincere thank you can make someone's day and strengthen your relationship with them.
- **Excuse Me:** A polite way to interrupt, apologize, or excuse yourself from a situation. Using this phrase appropriately shows that you're mindful of others and their comfort.

In my coaching practice, I've seen how these simple courtesies can transform interactions. Clients who made a conscious effort to incorporate "please," "thank you," and "excuse me" into their daily lives reported feeling more connected to others and more confident in their interactions. These words may be small, but their impact is profound.

Etiquette When on the Phone

Phone conversations require special attention to etiquette, as the absence of visual cues makes tone and language even more important:

- **Identify Yourself:** Always introduce yourself when making a call, especially if the person may not recognize your number. This simple step sets a professional tone and prevents confusion.
- **Speak Clearly and Politely:** Use a calm, clear voice and avoid interrupting. Clear communication is key to ensuring that your message is understood.
- **Respect the Other Person's Time:** Keep conversations concise and to the point, especially in professional settings. This shows that you value the other person's time and are mindful of their schedule.
- **Be Mindful of Your Surroundings:** Take calls in quiet, private spaces to avoid disturbing others. This consideration is especially important in shared spaces or public settings.
- **End the Call Politely:** Thank the person for their time and express your appreciation before hanging up. Ending a call on a positive note leaves a lasting impression.

Phone etiquette is a skill that many overlook, but it's crucial in today's fast-paced, often remote world. I've worked with clients who struggled with phone communication, whether due to nerves or lack of practice. By focusing on these key elements, they were able to improve their phone manners significantly, leading to better professional relationships and smoother interactions.

Practical Tips and Exercises

To help you put these principles and skills into practice, here are some exercises you can try in your daily life:

1. **Active Listening Exercise:** In your next conversation, focus on truly listening to the other person without planning your response while they're speaking. After they finish, summarize what they said to show you were paying attention. This exercise helps build empathy and shows respect for the speaker.

2. **Politeness Practice:** For one week, make a conscious effort to use "please," "thank you," and "excuse me" in all appropriate situations. Notice how these simple words influence your interactions. This practice can make a significant difference in how others perceive you and how you feel about your interactions.

3. **Introduction Role-Play:** Practice introducing yourself and others in different scenarios (e.g., formal business setting, casual social event) with a friend or family member. Focus on clarity, confidence, and context. Role-playing can help you become more comfortable with introductions, making them more natural and effective.

4. **Conversation Reflection:** After a conversation, reflect on how well you listened, how you responded, and whether you maintained a respectful and engaging tone. Identify one area to improve for next time. This reflection helps you become more aware of your conversation habits and how you can improve them.

5. **Phone Etiquette Check:** Pay attention to your phone manners during the next few calls. Ensure you're identifying yourself, speaking clearly, and respecting the other person's time. Practice ending calls with a polite, appreciative tone. Improving your phone etiquette can enhance your professional and personal relationships, making every call more effective.

Conclusion: Building a Foundation for Success

The Importance of Practicing Etiquette Daily

Good manners are not just for special occasions—they are the foundation of all our interactions. By consistently practicing respect, kindness, and empathy, you build a strong foundation for success in every area of your life. These principles, when applied daily, can transform your relationships and create a more positive environment for yourself and those around you.

The Ongoing Journey of Personal Growth

Learning and practicing etiquette is a lifelong journey. As you continue to refine your skills, you'll find that these principles become second nature, guiding you through even the most challenging situations with confidence and grace. My own experiences as a relationship coach have shown me that personal growth is a continuous process, and the more you invest in your social skills, the more rewarding your relationships will be.

Moving Forward with Confidence and Grace

As you progress through this book, remember that etiquette is about more than just following rules—it's about building meaningful connections and treating others with the respect and kindness they deserve. With each chapter, you'll gain new insights and tools to help you navigate the complexities of modern social life with confidence and grace. I encourage you to take these lessons to heart and apply them in your daily interactions, knowing that each step you take toward better etiquette brings you closer to a more fulfilling and harmonious life.

TWO

WORKPLACE ETIQUETTE

WORKPLACE ETIQUETTE PLAYS a critical role in shaping how we are perceived and how effectively we can collaborate with others. Professional manners extend beyond merely following rules; they are about demonstrating respect, integrity, and a commitment to fostering positive relationships in the workplace. Drawing from my two decades of experience as a relationship coach, I've seen how mastering workplace etiquette can elevate one's career and personal satisfaction. This chapter explores the key elements of workplace etiquette, covering first impressions, communication, and networking, with practical tips and exercises to help you refine your professional presence.

Professional Manners in the Workplace

The Importance of First Impressions in the Workplace

First impressions in the workplace are lasting and often set the tone for future interactions. Whether you're meeting a new client, attending a job interview, or introducing yourself to a new colleague, the impression you make in those first few moments can significantly influence how others perceive your professionalism and competence.

Creating a positive first impression involves more than just what you say; it includes your body language, attire, punctuality, and overall demeanor. A firm handshake, eye contact, and a genuine smile can convey confidence and approachability. Being well-prepared, attentive, and courteous will further enhance the positive impression you make.

Over the years, I've coached many professionals who struggled with making strong first impressions. I've seen how a little guidance in areas like body language and conversational skills can completely change the trajectory of their careers. It's about presenting your best self from the very beginning, setting the stage for success in every professional interaction.

Dress Code and Grooming: Modern Expectations

Dress codes in the workplace can vary widely depending on the industry, company culture, and geographical location. However, dressing appropriately is a fundamental aspect of workplace etiquette, as it reflects your understanding of the professional environment and your respect for those you work with.

- **Traditional Business Attire:** In more formal industries such as finance, law, or consulting, a traditional business suit, tie, and polished shoes for men, and a tailored dress or suit for women, are typically expected.
- **Business Casual:** In many modern workplaces, business casual is the norm. This might include slacks or skirts paired with a blouse, button-down shirt, or a smart sweater. Avoid overly casual items like jeans, t-shirts, or sneakers unless explicitly allowed.
- **Grooming:** Neat grooming is essential regardless of the dress code. Pay attention to details such as clean and styled hair, well-maintained nails, and minimal, professional makeup. A tidy appearance conveys that you take your role seriously and respect the professional environment.

Throughout my career, I've observed how dressing appropriately can significantly impact how others perceive you. It's not about being the most fashionable person in the room but about showing that you understand the culture and expectations of your workplace. This understanding can boost your confidence and help you feel more integrated into your professional environment.

Punctuality, Reliability, and Respecting Others' Time

Punctuality is a clear indicator of your respect for others and your commitment to your responsibilities. Arriving on time—or ideally a few minutes early—for meetings, appointments, and deadlines shows that you value others' time and are reliable.

In addition to being punctual, consistently delivering on your promises and meeting deadlines is crucial. Reliability builds trust and reinforces your reputation as a dependable professional. If you're running late or unable to meet a deadline, communicate proactively to manage expectations and find a solution.

I've worked with clients who struggled with time management, and I've seen how small changes—like setting reminders or planning your day in advance—can lead to significant improvements in their professional relationships. Punctuality and reliability are not just about being on time; they are about respecting others and being someone others can count on.

Communication Etiquette

Effective and Polite Email Communication

Email is one of the most common forms of communication in the workplace, and how you use it reflects your professionalism. Here are some key guidelines for effective and polite email communication:

- **Clear Subject Lines:** Always use a subject line that accurately reflects the content of your email. This helps the recipient prioritize and organize their emails.

- **Professional Salutations and Closures:** Start your emails with a polite greeting (e.g., "Dear Mr. Smith," or "Hello Jane,") and end with a courteous closing (e.g., "Best regards," or "Sincerely,").
- **Concise and Clear Content:** Be clear and to the point. Use bullet points or numbered lists to break up large blocks of text and ensure that your message is easy to read and understand.
- **Respond Promptly:** Aim to respond to emails within 24 hours, even if it's just to acknowledge receipt and let the sender know when you'll provide a more detailed response.
- **Proofread Before Sending:** Always check your emails for spelling and grammatical errors before hitting send. A well-written email reflects attention to detail and professionalism.

In my coaching practice, I've seen how mastering email etiquette can transform a professional's reputation. One client, who was frequently misunderstood in email communications, learned to be more concise and polite in his messaging. The result was not only improved relationships with colleagues but also increased respect from his peers and supervisors.

The Do's and Don'ts of Phone and Video Calls

Phone and video calls are integral to modern business communication, especially in an era of remote work. Proper etiquette in these contexts is essential for maintaining professionalism.

- **Phone Calls:**
- **Do:** Introduce yourself at the start of the call, especially if you're not sure the other person has your contact details. Speak clearly and listen actively, taking notes if necessary.
- **Don't:** Avoid interrupting the other person. Wait for a natural pause before contributing. Also, refrain from multitasking during the call, as it can be distracting and disrespectful.
- **Video Calls:**

- **Do:** Ensure your background is tidy and professional. Dress appropriately, even if the call is from home. Make sure your camera and microphone are working properly before the call starts.
- **Don't:** Avoid checking your phone or other devices during the call. Additionally, don't forget to mute your microphone when you're not speaking to avoid background noise.

I remember working with a client who struggled with video calls during the shift to remote work. By focusing on these basics—like creating a professional environment and practicing clear communication—she was able to overcome her initial discomfort and excel in this new medium.

Navigating Social Media in a Professional Context

Social media can blur the lines between personal and professional life, so it's important to navigate these platforms with care.

- **Professionalism on LinkedIn:** LinkedIn is a professional network, so ensure your profile reflects your career aspirations. Share relevant industry news, engage with colleagues' posts in a respectful manner, and avoid controversial topics.
- **Privacy Settings on Other Platforms:** On platforms like Facebook, Instagram, or Twitter, be mindful of what you post. Adjust privacy settings to control who can see your content, and avoid posting anything that could damage your professional reputation.
- **Consistency Across Platforms:** Your online persona should align with your professional identity. Inconsistent or inappropriate content can harm your credibility.

Over the years, I've seen how social media can either enhance or detract from a professional's image. I've advised clients to regularly audit their online presence, ensuring that their profiles reflect their values and professional goals. This consistency builds a strong, trust-worthy personal brand.

Proper Behavior in Meetings and Conferences

Meetings are a staple of business life, and how you conduct yourself in these settings speaks volumes about your professionalism.

- **Preparation:** Arrive prepared, having reviewed any relevant materials in advance. Bring a notebook or device to take notes.
- **Participation:** Engage actively but respectfully. Contribute when appropriate, but avoid dominating the conversation. Be concise and to the point when speaking.
- **Body Language:** Maintain good posture, make eye contact, and show attentiveness. Avoid distracting behaviors such as fidgeting or checking your phone.
- **Follow-Up:** After the meeting, follow up with any action items or a summary email if appropriate. This demonstrates your commitment and reliability.

I've worked with many clients who felt overwhelmed by meetings, unsure of how to contribute effectively. By focusing on preparation and participation, they were able to build confidence and become more valued members of their teams.

How to Network Gracefully and Build Professional Relationships

Networking is a key component of career development, and doing it well requires a balance of confidence and courtesy.

- **Introduction Techniques:** When introducing yourself, provide a brief but engaging summary of who you are and what you do. Offer a firm handshake and maintain eye contact.

- **Business Cards:** Always have business cards handy, and exchange them with a brief conversation. When receiving a card, take a moment to read it before putting it away, showing respect for the person's details.
- **Follow-Up:** After meeting someone new, follow up with a polite email or LinkedIn connection request, referencing your conversation and expressing your interest in staying in touch.

Networking can be daunting, especially for those new to the professional world. I've helped many clients develop their networking skills by practicing introductions and follow-ups, which has led to new opportunities and stronger professional relationships.

Business Dining Etiquette: Hosting and Attending with Style

Business meals are often where important relationships and deals are cultivated. Understanding dining etiquette is crucial to making a positive impression.

- **Hosting a Meal:** As the host, it's your responsibility to make reservations, arrive early, and handle the check discreetly. Guide the conversation, ensuring it stays professional yet pleasant.
- **Attending a Meal:** If you're a guest, arrive on time and dress appropriately. Follow the lead of the host regarding menu choices and conversation topics. Express gratitude at the end of the meal.
- **Table Manners:** Familiarize yourself with the basics of table settings, utensil use, and meal pacing. Avoid discussing overly personal or controversial topics, and always thank the host before leaving.

I've seen how business meals can either solidify a professional relationship or, if handled poorly, create tension. I've coached clients on the finer points of dining etiquette, helping them feel more comfortable and confident in these settings. A successful business meal can be a powerful tool for career advancement.

Practical Tips and Exercises

To help you refine your workplace etiquette, here are some practical tips and exercises:

1. **First Impressions Exercise:** For the next week, consciously focus on making strong first impressions. Pay attention to your handshake, eye contact, and initial conversation. Reflect on how others respond and note any areas for improvement.
2. **Email Review:** Go through your recent work emails and evaluate them against the guidelines provided. Consider whether your subject lines are clear, your tone is professional, and if your emails are concise. Make adjustments as necessary.
3. **Video Call Setup:** Assess your video call environment. Check your background, lighting, and camera angle to ensure they present a professional image. Practice a mock video call to see how you appear on screen.
4. **Networking Role-Play:** Practice your networking skills with a friend or colleague. Role-play introducing yourself at a networking event, exchanging business cards, and following up afterward. Focus on confidence, clarity, and courtesy.
5. **Dining Etiquette Drill:** If possible, attend a business lunch or dinner and apply the dining etiquette tips. If not, practice at home by setting a formal table and going through the motions of a business meal, paying attention to pacing, conversation, and utensil use.

By integrating these exercises into your routine, you'll develop a stronger grasp of workplace etiquette, enabling you to navigate the professional world with confidence and respect.

The Importance of Consistency in Professional Etiquette

Mastering workplace etiquette is about more than just following rules; it's about understanding the principles that underlie professional interactions and applying them consistently. Whether you're crafting a well-worded email, participating in a meeting, or networking with industry peers, your attention to detail and respect for others will set you apart as a polished and competent professional. Over the years, I've seen how consistency in these areas can lead to greater opportunities, stronger relationships, and a more fulfilling career.

The Role of Etiquette in Career Success

In my 20 years as a relationship coach, I've watched clients transform their careers simply by honing their workplace etiquette. It's not just about knowing what to do; it's about applying these skills with intention and empathy. Your professional etiquette reflects your values, your commitment to excellence, and your respect for the people you work with. These are the qualities that will help you build a reputation for integrity and reliability, setting you on a path to long-term success.

Moving Forward with Confidence

As you continue through this guide, you'll delve into other important areas of modern etiquette, including how to engage respectfully and inclusively with diverse and marginalized communities. These skills will not only enhance your professional life but will also enrich your personal interactions, helping you to build a reputation for integrity, empathy, and excellence. I encourage you to take these lessons to heart, apply them in your daily interactions, and watch as your professional relationships and opportunities flourish.

THREE

ETIQUETTE FOR MEN

IN A WORLD that is constantly evolving, so too are the expectations and norms surrounding male behavior. Etiquette for men today involves striking a balance between respecting traditional values and embracing modern ideals of equality and inclusivity. Throughout my 20 years as a relationship coach, I've seen how men can navigate social and professional settings with confidence, respect, and style, and I've guided countless individuals toward becoming their best selves in all interactions. This chapter explores how men can embody these qualities, providing practical advice on everything from dressing for success to handling conflicts in male-dominated environments.

Modern Manners for Men

The Balance Between Traditional Chivalry and Modern Equality

Chivalry, traditionally associated with acts of courtesy such as opening doors, offering seats, or paying for meals, has long been a hallmark of gentlemanly behavior. However, in today's society, it's important to balance these gestures with a respect for modern ideals of equality.

For instance, offering to carry someone's bags or opening a door can still be seen as polite, but it's essential to do so without implying that the person is incapable or inferior. The key is to approach these acts as gestures of kindness and respect, not as obligations or displays of superiority. Always be attentive to how the gesture is received, and be willing to adapt your behavior to make others feel comfortable and respected.

In my work, I've often coached men who were unsure of how to reconcile traditional chivalry with modern expectations. The key, I've found, is mindfulness—being aware of how your actions are perceived and being open to adapting your behavior. This approach ensures that your chivalrous actions are seen as respectful and considerate, rather than outdated or condescending.

Dressing for Success: Understanding Modern Dress Codes

Your attire is one of the first things people notice about you, and dressing appropriately can greatly influence how you're perceived in both social and professional settings. Understanding and adhering to dress codes is crucial for making a positive impression.

- **Business Formal:** In traditional corporate settings, a well-tailored suit in neutral colors, paired with a crisp dress shirt, tie, and polished shoes, is the standard. Accessories should be kept minimal and tasteful.
- **Business Casual:** Many modern workplaces have adopted a business casual dress code, which allows for more flexibility. This might include slacks or chinos, a button-down shirt, and loafers or dress shoes. Ties are often optional, but the overall look should still be polished.
- **Casual Settings:** For social events, casual attire can range from smart-casual (e.g., a collared shirt with jeans) to completely informal (e.g., t-shirts and shorts). Even in casual settings, it's important to dress neatly and appropriately for the occasion.

I've guided many men through wardrobe transformations, helping them understand that dressing well is not just about fashion—it's about respect. Respect for the occasion, the people you're with, and yourself. When you dress appropriately, you send a message that you are aware of your environment and that you value the people around you.

Navigating Social Interactions with Confidence and Respect

Confidence and respect are the cornerstones of successful social interactions. Whether you're meeting someone for the first time, attending a social event, or engaging in a professional discussion, how you present yourself matters.

- **Body Language:** Stand tall, make eye contact, and offer a firm handshake. These nonverbal cues convey confidence and openness.
- **Communication:** Speak clearly and listen actively. Avoid interrupting others, and show genuine interest in what they have to say. Polite conversation involves a balance between speaking and listening, ensuring that everyone feels heard and respected.
- **Respecting Boundaries:** Always be mindful of personal space and cultural differences. What is acceptable in one context may not be in another, so it's important to adapt your behavior accordingly.

In my years of coaching, I've often helped men develop their social confidence by focusing on these basics. The result is always transformative—when you exude confidence and respect, others naturally respond with the same, leading to more meaningful and positive interactions.

Etiquette in Male-Dominated Environments

How to Maintain Professionalism and Courtesy in Competitive Settings

Male-dominated environments, such as certain industries or sports, can sometimes foster a competitive atmosphere. While healthy competition can be motivating, it's crucial to maintain professionalism and courtesy at all times.

- **Respect for Colleagues:** Treat everyone with respect, regardless of their position or background. Acknowledge others' contributions and successes, and avoid undermining or belittling others to get ahead.
- **Constructive Feedback:** When offering feedback, focus on constructive criticism rather than harsh judgment. Approach conversations with the intent to help others improve rather than to assert dominance.
- **Collaboration Over Competition:** Foster a collaborative environment where teamwork is valued over individual competition. This not only enhances productivity but also builds stronger relationships among colleagues.

I've seen how men can sometimes struggle with balancing competition and collaboration. In my coaching practice, I emphasize the importance of lifting others up rather than tearing them down. This approach not only creates a more positive work environment but also enhances your reputation as a leader and a team player.

Respecting Diversity and Promoting Inclusivity

In today's workplace, diversity and inclusion are more important than ever. As a professional, it's essential to promote inclusivity and respect the diverse backgrounds and perspectives of your colleagues.

- **Cultural Sensitivity:** Be aware of cultural differences and avoid making assumptions based on stereotypes. Educate yourself about the cultural backgrounds of your colleagues to better understand their perspectives.
- **Inclusive Language:** Use language that is inclusive and respectful. Avoid jokes or comments that could be offensive

or discriminatory. If you're unsure whether something is appropriate, err on the side of caution.

- **Support for Diversity Initiatives:** Actively support initiatives that promote diversity and inclusion in your workplace. This could involve participating in diversity training, joining employee resource groups, or advocating for inclusive policies.

Throughout my career, I've worked with many men who wanted to be more inclusive but weren't sure how to start. The first step, I often say, is awareness. Once you're aware of the importance of diversity and inclusion, the rest—learning, adapting, supporting—will follow naturally.

Handling Disagreements and Conflicts with Tact

Disagreements are inevitable in any environment, but how you handle them can significantly impact your professional relationships and reputation.

- **Stay Calm and Composed:** When a disagreement arises, stay calm and composed. Avoid raising your voice or becoming confrontational. Instead, focus on finding a resolution through calm and rational discussion.
- **Listen to Understand:** Before responding, listen carefully to the other person's perspective. Understanding their point of view can help you find common ground and work towards a solution.
- **Focus on the Issue, Not the Person:** Keep the discussion focused on the issue at hand rather than making it personal. Avoid blaming or attacking the other person, and instead, work together to find a constructive solution.

In my experience, many conflicts can be resolved—or avoided altogether—by focusing on understanding rather than winning. I've coached men through difficult workplace conflicts, helping them learn to de-escalate situations with tact and empathy, which often leads to stronger, more respectful relationships.

Social Etiquette for Men

Hosting and Attending Events with Style

Whether you're hosting a dinner party or attending a social gathering, your behavior can greatly influence the success of the event and your reputation as a gentleman.

- **Hosting:**
- **Preparation:** Plan your event carefully, considering the comfort and preferences of your guests. Send out invitations in advance, and make sure your home or venue is clean and welcoming.
- **Hospitality:** Greet each guest personally, offer them refreshments, and make introductions if necessary. Ensure that everyone feels included and comfortable throughout the event.
- **Gratitude:** After the event, thank your guests for coming, either in person or with a follow-up message. A handwritten note can add a personal touch.
- **Attending:**
- **Punctuality:** Arrive on time, or if you're running late, notify the host. Bringing a small gift, such as a bottle of wine or a bouquet of flowers, is a thoughtful gesture.
- **Engagement:** Participate actively in conversations, introduce yourself to new people, and show appreciation for the host's efforts.
- **Thanking the Host:** Before leaving, thank the host for their hospitality. A follow-up message or note the next day is also a considerate way to express your gratitude.

I've always enjoyed helping men refine their hosting and attending skills because these are opportunities to truly connect with others.

Whether through a well-planned event or a thoughtful thank-you note, these gestures of hospitality and gratitude can leave a lasting impression and strengthen your social bonds.

The Gentleman's Guide to Dating and Relationships

Dating and relationships require a balance of confidence, respect, and genuine care. Here's how to navigate them with the grace of a true gentleman:

- **First Impressions:** When meeting someone for the first time, whether on a date or in a relationship setting, make a positive first impression by being punctual, well-groomed, and attentive.
- **Respecting Boundaries:** Respect your date's personal boundaries and pace the relationship according to mutual comfort levels. Consent and communication are key in any relationship.
- **Chivalry with Equality:** While traditional gestures like opening doors or paying for meals can still be appreciated, ensure that your actions come from a place of kindness rather than obligation. Always consider your partner's preferences and be open to shared responsibilities.

I've guided many men through the intricacies of dating and relationships, emphasizing that respect and communication are the foundations of any successful relationship. The balance between chivalry and equality is not always easy, but when done right, it leads to more meaningful and fulfilling connections.

Sportsmanship: Manners in Competitive Environments

Sports and other competitive environments are where your manners are often put to the test. Good sportsmanship is about more than just playing by the rules—it's about respecting your opponents, teammates, and the spirit of the game.

- **Respect for Opponents:** Whether you win or lose, always show respect for your opponents. Shake hands after the game, congratulate them on their performance, and avoid trash-talking or gloating.

- **Teamwork:** In team sports, support your teammates, celebrate their successes, and offer encouragement during challenging moments. Avoid blaming others for mistakes and focus on constructive feedback.
- **Grace in Winning and Losing:** Handle both victory and defeat with grace. When you win, celebrate modestly, and when you lose, accept it graciously and use it as an opportunity to learn and improve.

As someone who has coached men through both personal and professional challenges, I've seen how sportsmanship extends beyond the playing field. The principles of respect, humility, and grace in competition are just as important in the workplace and in life. They build character and earn respect from others.

Practical Tips and Exercises

To help you refine your etiquette as a modern gentleman, here are some practical tips and exercises:

1. **Chivalry in Practice:** Over the next week, consciously incorporate acts of chivalry into your daily routine, such as holding doors open, offering your seat, or carrying bags. Pay attention to how these gestures are received and adjust your approach based on feedback.
2. **Dress Code Audit:** Review your wardrobe to ensure you have appropriate attire for different dress codes (business formal, business casual, and casual). Identify any gaps and plan to invest in key pieces that will enhance your professional image.
3. **Conflict Resolution Role-Play:** Practice handling disagreements with a friend or colleague through role-playing. Focus on staying calm, listening actively, and

resolving the issue respectfully. Reflect on how you can apply these skills in real-life situations.

4. **Event Hosting Practice:** Host a small gathering for friends or colleagues, focusing on planning, hospitality, and post-event gratitude. Use this as an opportunity to practice the etiquette of hosting and to receive feedback from your guests.

5. **Dating Etiquette Reflection:** Reflect on your recent dating experiences or relationships. Consider how well you've respected boundaries, communicated effectively, and balanced chivalry with equality. Identify areas where you can improve and plan how to apply these insights moving forward.

By consistently practicing these tips and exercises, you'll strengthen your etiquette skills, helping you navigate social and professional environments with confidence, respect, and style.

Conclusion: The Modern Gentleman's Path

Balancing Tradition and Modernity

Mastering modern etiquette as a man involves balancing traditional values with contemporary expectations. It's about knowing when to uphold traditions and when to adapt to modern ideals of equality and respect. Through my years of coaching, I've seen how men who embrace this balance not only gain respect from others but also find greater satisfaction in their personal and professional lives.

The Impact of Good Etiquette on Relationships

Whether you're dressing for success, navigating competitive environments, or building relationships, the principles of respect, kindness, and inclusivity are essential. These are not just abstract concepts—they are the foundations of every positive interaction. I've seen first-hand how men who cultivate these qualities experience deeper connections and more rewarding relationships, both at work and in their personal lives.

Continuing the Journey of Personal Growth

As you continue through this guide, you'll explore etiquette in other important areas, including how to engage respectfully and inclusively with diverse and marginalized communities. These skills will not only enhance your social and professional life but will also help you build a reputation as a gentleman who embodies integrity, empathy, and excellence. I encourage you to embrace these lessons, continue refining your etiquette, and take pride in the growth you'll experience along the way.

FOUR

ETIQUETTE FOR WOMEN

THE CONCEPT of etiquette for women has expanded to encompass both the preservation of timeless manners and the embrace of modern values. Women are expected to navigate a variety of social and professional settings with grace, confidence, and sophistication. Over my 20 years as a relationship coach, I've seen how mastering the balance between tradition and modernity empowers women to shine in any situation. This chapter explores how women can maintain poise, dress with elegance, and build meaningful relationships in both female-dominated environments and broader social contexts.

Modern Manners for Women

Balancing Tradition and Modernity in Social Interactions

The art of balancing tradition with modernity is key to navigating social interactions as a woman in today's world. While traditional manners such as politeness, respect, and consideration remain relevant, modern values such as equality, independence, and inclusivity are equally important.

- **Politeness and Assertiveness:** Traditional etiquette often emphasizes politeness and deference, which remain valuable traits. However, in modern contexts, it's also important to be assertive—expressing your opinions and standing your ground while maintaining respect for others.

- **Respecting Choices:** In social interactions, respect the diverse choices and lifestyles of those around you. Whether it's decisions about career, family, or personal life, acknowledging and supporting others' choices reflects a modern, inclusive approach to etiquette.
- **Adaptability:** The ability to adapt your behavior to suit different contexts—whether traditional or modern—is crucial. For example, you might adopt more formal manners in a traditional setting while embracing a more relaxed approach in a modern, casual environment.

In my coaching practice, I've worked with many women who have struggled to find this balance. The key, I've found, is to remain authentic while being adaptable. Whether you're navigating a corporate boardroom or a casual social event, staying true to your values while being considerate of others' expectations allows you to move confidently between different social settings.

Dressing with Elegance: Understanding Contemporary Dress Codes

Dressing appropriately for various occasions is an essential aspect of modern etiquette for women. Your attire should reflect the event, setting, and your personal style, while also conveying professionalism and respect.

- **Business Formal:** In corporate settings, a well-tailored suit, sheath dress, or coordinated skirt and blouse in neutral or dark tones is often expected. Pair with understated accessories and closed-toe shoes for a polished look.
- **Business Casual:** Many workplaces allow for business casual attire, which offers more flexibility. Consider tailored trousers, a blouse, and loafers or flats. Dresses and skirts

should be of an appropriate length, and avoid overly casual items like jeans or sneakers unless specified.

- **Casual and Social Events:** For casual settings, you can express more of your personal style. Smart-casual outfits might include well-fitted jeans with a stylish top and flats or ankle boots. For more formal social events, a cocktail dress or a well-chosen ensemble that reflects the occasion's tone is appropriate.

Throughout my career, I've helped women develop a wardrobe that aligns with both their professional goals and personal expression. Dressing with elegance isn't about following rigid rules but about finding what makes you feel confident and comfortable, while also respecting the context of the situation.

Navigating Social and Professional Settings with Poise

Poise is the ability to carry yourself with grace and confidence, regardless of the setting. It involves maintaining a calm and composed demeanor, even in challenging situations.

- **Body Language:** Good posture, eye contact, and a warm smile are key elements of poise. These nonverbal cues convey confidence and approachability, making you more effective in social and professional interactions.
- **Communication:** Speak clearly and confidently, but also listen attentively to others. A poised woman balances her communication by being assertive when necessary, yet always respectful and considerate of others' perspectives.
- **Handling Challenges:** When faced with difficult situations, maintain your composure. Whether dealing with a rude comment or a stressful scenario, staying calm and responding thoughtfully will reflect your poise and professionalism.

I've witnessed how poise can transform a woman's presence in any environment. It's not just about what you say or wear; it's about how you carry yourself. Women who cultivate poise tend to command respect and build stronger, more positive relationships.

Maintaining Professionalism and Camaraderie

In female-dominated environments, whether in the workplace or social settings, it's important to balance professionalism with camaraderie. Women often excel in creating supportive, collaborative environments, but it's crucial to maintain professional boundaries to ensure a respectful and productive atmosphere.

- **Respecting Boundaries:** While camaraderie is valuable, always be mindful of maintaining professional boundaries. Avoid oversharing personal information in a professional setting and respect others' privacy.
- **Collaborative Leadership:** Women often lead with a collaborative approach, fostering teamwork and mutual support. Encourage open communication, share credit for successes, and support your colleagues' development.
- **Dealing with Cliques:** In some female-dominated environments, cliques can form, which may lead to exclusionary behavior. Strive to be inclusive, reaching out to all members of the group and promoting a sense of unity.

In my experience, women thrive in environments where they feel both supported and respected. I've seen how creating a balance between camaraderie and professionalism can lead to more productive and harmonious workplaces, where everyone feels valued and included.

Building Supportive Networks and Mentoring Relationships

Networking and mentoring are powerful tools for professional and personal growth. In female-dominated environments, building supportive networks and fostering mentoring relationships can help women advance their careers and navigate challenges.

- **Networking:** Attend industry events, join professional organizations, and participate in online forums to connect with other women in your field. Networking is not just about exchanging business cards—it's about building genuine relationships that can offer mutual support and opportunities.
- **Mentorship:** Whether you are a mentor or mentee, these relationships can be invaluable. As a mentee, seek out mentors who can offer guidance, advice, and encouragement. As a mentor, share your experiences, offer support, and help guide others in their professional journeys.
- **Supporting Each Other:** Women supporting women is a powerful force. Advocate for your female colleagues, celebrate their successes, and stand together in the face of challenges.

I've had the privilege of mentoring many women throughout my career, and I've seen how these relationships can make a profound difference. A strong network of supportive women can provide the encouragement and resources needed to overcome obstacles and achieve great things.

Handling Competition and Conflict Gracefully

In any professional environment, competition and conflict are inevitable. Handling these situations with grace is essential for maintaining a positive and productive atmosphere.

- **Healthy Competition:** Competition can be motivating when approached positively. Focus on personal growth and improvement rather than comparing yourself to others. Celebrate others' successes as well as your own.
- **Conflict Resolution:** When conflicts arise, address them

directly but respectfully. Approach the situation with a problem-solving mindset, seeking to understand the other person's perspective and finding a mutually agreeable solution.

- **Avoiding Gossip:** Gossip can be detrimental to professional relationships and workplace morale. Refrain from engaging in gossip and instead focus on constructive communication that fosters trust and respect.

I've coached many women through the challenges of workplace competition and conflict. The key, I've found, is to maintain your integrity and focus on solutions rather than problems. This approach not only helps resolve conflicts but also builds your reputation as a fair and capable leader.

Social Etiquette for Women

Hosting and Attending Events with Sophistication

Whether you're hosting a dinner party or attending a social gathering, your behavior sets the tone for the event and reflects your personal etiquette.

- **Hosting:**
- **Planning and Preparation:** Plan your event with attention to detail, considering your guests' preferences and dietary restrictions. Send out invitations well in advance and prepare your home or venue to create a welcoming atmosphere.
- **Greeting Guests:** Personally greet each guest upon arrival, offer them refreshments, and introduce them to others if needed. Ensure that everyone feels included and comfortable throughout the event.
- **Graceful Hosting:** During the event, engage with your guests, keep the conversation flowing, and ensure that everyone is enjoying themselves. After the event, thank your

guests for coming and follow up with a personal note of gratitude if appropriate.

- **Attending:**
- **Punctuality:** Arrive on time or a few minutes early. If you're bringing a guest, make sure they are also aware of the event's expectations and etiquette.
- **Gifts:** It's customary to bring a small gift for the host, such as flowers, wine, or a thoughtful item that reflects the host's interests.
- **Engagement:** Participate in conversations, show interest in others, and be a gracious guest. Before leaving, thank the host personally for their hospitality.

In my years of coaching, I've seen how hosting and attending events with sophistication can significantly impact one's social standing and relationships. It's not just about following etiquette—it's about creating meaningful experiences for yourself and others.

The Modern Woman's Guide to Dating and Relationships

Dating and relationships today require a blend of traditional etiquette and modern values. Whether you're dating or in a long-term relationship, how you conduct yourself reflects your respect for both yourself and your partner.

- **First Impressions:** Make a positive first impression by being punctual, well-groomed, and attentive. Show interest in your date by asking questions and listening actively.
- **Respecting Boundaries:** Respect your own boundaries and those of your partner. Communicate openly about your needs and expectations, and ensure that the relationship progresses at a pace that's comfortable for both parties.
- **Balancing Tradition and Modernity:** Traditional gestures such as offering to pay for a meal or holding a door open can still be appreciated, but they should be offered in a spirit of kindness and equality. Be open to sharing responsibilities and decision-making in the relationship.

I've guided many women through the intricacies of dating, emphasizing that respect, communication, and balance are the keys to a
successful relationship. It's important to remain true to your values
while being open to the dynamics of modern relationships.

Etiquette in Volunteer Work and Community Involvement

Volunteer work and community involvement are rewarding ways to
contribute to society. Maintaining proper etiquette in these roles
ensures that your contributions are respectful, effective, and
appreciated.

- **Commitment and Reliability:** When you commit to
  volunteer work, treat it with the same seriousness as any
  other professional obligation. Show up on time, follow
  through on your commitments, and communicate
  proactively if you need to reschedule or change your
  availability.
- **Respect for All:** In community work, you'll interact with
  people from diverse backgrounds. Approach these
  interactions with an open mind, respect for differences, and
  a willingness to learn.
- **Collaboration and Teamwork:** Volunteer work often
  involves collaboration. Be a supportive team member, listen
  to others' ideas, and contribute positively to the group's
  efforts.

I've always encouraged women to engage in volunteer work as a way
to give back and build community connections. The relationships
and experiences gained through volunteering are invaluable and can
greatly enrich your personal and professional life.

Practical Tips and Exercises

To help you refine your etiquette as a modern woman, here are some
practical tips and exercises:

1. **Balancing Tradition and Modernity:** Reflect on how you balance traditional and modern manners in your daily interactions. Over the next week, practice incorporating assertiveness into situations where you might traditionally defer, such as voicing your opinion in meetings or making decisions in social settings.

2. **Dress Code Evaluation:** Take a day to evaluate your wardrobe in relation to your professional and social activities. Identify areas where you can enhance your attire to better align with contemporary dress codes, and consider investing in versatile pieces that can be dressed up or down.

3. **Networking Practice:** Identify an upcoming event where you can practice your networking skills. Set a goal to meet at least three new people, introduce yourself confidently, and follow up with them afterward. Reflect on how these interactions can help you build supportive networks.

4. **Conflict Resolution Exercise:** Think of a recent situation where you experienced competition or conflict. Role-play a similar scenario with a friend, focusing on using respectful language, staying calm, and finding a constructive solution. Apply these skills the next time a real-life conflict arises.

5. **Volunteer Commitment:** If you're involved in volunteer work, review your commitments and ensure you're meeting them reliably. If you're not currently volunteering, consider finding an opportunity that aligns with your values and practice the etiquette of community involvement.

By consistently practicing these tips and exercises, you'll strengthen your etiquette skills, allowing you to navigate social and professional environments with confidence, elegance, and respect.

Conclusion: The Essence of Modern Etiquette for Women

Balancing Timeless Traditions with Modern Values

Mastering etiquette as a modern woman involves a delicate balance between upholding timeless traditions and embracing contemporary values. It's about knowing when to rely on the wisdom of the past and when to adapt to the demands of the present. Over the years, I've seen how women who navigate this balance effectively not only command respect but also lead more fulfilling lives.

The Power of Poise and Grace

In both social and professional settings, poise and grace are your greatest assets. These qualities allow you to handle any situation with confidence and elegance. Whether you're leading a team, attending a social event, or building a relationship, your ability to remain composed and considerate will set you apart. I've watched countless women grow in their personal and professional lives by embracing these principles, and I know you can too.

Continuing Your Journey of Personal Growth

As you continue through this guide, you'll explore more areas of modern etiquette, including how to navigate diverse and inclusive environments with respect and understanding. These skills will not only enhance your social and professional life but also help you build a reputation as a woman of integrity, empathy, and excellence. I encourage you to embrace these lessons, apply them in your daily life, and take pride in the person you are becoming. The journey of personal growth is ongoing, and with each step, you become more equipped to face the world with grace, confidence, and an unshake-able sense of self.

FIVE

GENDER ETIQUETTE

IN OUR INCREASINGLY DIVERSE and interconnected world, understanding and respecting gender diversity and sexual orientation is essential for fostering inclusive and supportive environments. This chapter provides guidance for cis-gendered and heterosexual individuals on navigating interactions with people of diverse gender identities and sexual orientations. Additionally, it offers advice for individuals from gender and sexuality diverse communities on interacting with traditional gender identities and sexualities. The goal is to promote understanding, respect, and positive communication in all social interactions.

Introduction: Understanding Gender Diversity and Sexual Orientation

The Evolution of Gender and Sexuality

Gender and sexuality have always been integral aspects of human identity, but societal understanding of these concepts has evolved significantly over time. Traditionally, gender was viewed through a binary lens—male and female—closely tied to biological sex. Similarly, sexual orientation was often seen in terms of heterosexuality as the norm, with other orientations marginalized or stigmatized.

However, in recent decades, there has been a growing recognition that both gender and sexuality exist on spectrums, encompassing a wide range of identities and expressions. This shift has led to greater visibility and acceptance of diverse gender identities, such as transgender, non-binary, and genderqueer, as well as a broader understanding of sexual orientations beyond heterosexuality, including lesbian, gay, bisexual, asexual, and others.

In my 20 years of coaching, I've seen how this evolution has impacted the way we interact with one another. I've witnessed the struggles of those who felt confined by traditional definitions and the relief and empowerment that came with the broader acceptance of diverse identities. It's a reminder that our understanding of identity is ever-changing, and so too must be our approach to interacting with others.

Why Gender Etiquette Matters

Gender etiquette plays a crucial role in promoting inclusivity and respect in our interactions with others. By practicing good gender etiquette, we acknowledge and affirm the identities of those around us, helping to create environments where everyone feels valued and respected. Misunderstanding or ignoring someone's gender identity or sexual orientation can lead to discomfort, exclusion, or even harm. Thus, understanding and applying gender etiquette is not just a matter of politeness—it's a way of fostering equality and understanding in society.

I've often reflected on how small acts of recognition—like using someone's correct pronouns—can have a profound impact. These gestures of respect build bridges and foster trust, and I've seen them transform environments from places of tension to spaces of acceptance.

Navigating Gender and Sexual Diversity for Cis-Gendered and Heterosexual Individuals

Respectful Communication

Communication is key to respectful interactions, and using the correct pronouns and names is a fundamental aspect of gender etiquette. When meeting someone new, it's respectful to ask for their pronouns if they aren't offered, and to use them consistently. For example, you might say, "Hi, I'm Alex. My pronouns are he/him. What about you?" This approach normalizes the sharing of pronouns and shows that you're committed to respecting their identity.

It's also important to avoid making assumptions about someone's gender based on their appearance or behavior. Instead of guessing, always ask when in doubt, and listen carefully to how people introduce themselves. This not only shows respect but also fosters an environment where everyone's identity is acknowledged.

Throughout my career, I've seen how transformative respectful communication can be. I remember working with a client who was nervous about asking for someone's pronouns, fearing they might offend. But once they practiced it, they found it opened doors to more honest and meaningful conversations.

Understanding and Using Inclusive Language

Inclusive language is another vital component of gender etiquette. Language evolves, and staying informed about the terms and phrases that are considered respectful is crucial. For instance, using "partner" instead of "husband" or "wife" when referring to someone's significant other is a more inclusive way to acknowledge diverse relationships.

Gender-neutral terms are also important in everyday conversations. For example, instead of saying "ladies and gentlemen," you might say "everyone" or "folks." These small adjustments can make a significant difference in making all individuals feel included.

In my own life, I've had to unlearn certain phrases and adopt new ones. It's a process that requires mindfulness, but the rewards—seeing others feel recognized and respected—make it worth the effort.

Creating Inclusive Spaces

Creating inclusive spaces—whether in the workplace, social groups, or public events—requires thoughtful consideration of the needs of gender and sexuality diverse individuals. This can include offering gender-neutral restrooms, using inclusive language in invitations, and ensuring that events are accessible and welcoming to all.

Being an ally is also an important aspect of creating inclusive spaces. This involves not only supporting gender and sexuality diverse individuals but also advocating for their rights and inclusion in various settings. Allies can play a significant role in challenging discriminatory behaviors and promoting a culture of respect and inclusivity.

I've been fortunate to witness the power of inclusive spaces firsthand. I recall a client who implemented gender-neutral restrooms at their workplace, which led to a noticeable shift in the company culture—people felt safer, more respected, and more willing to bring their full selves to work.

Addressing Mistakes with Grace

Everyone makes mistakes, and the key to maintaining respect and trust is how you handle them. If you use the wrong pronoun or make a mistake in addressing someone's gender or orientation, it's important to apologize sincerely and correct yourself without making a big deal out of it. For example, if you mistakenly use the wrong pronoun, a simple "I'm sorry, I meant they" followed by moving on with the conversation is often the best approach.

Learning from mistakes is part of the process. Take the opportunity to educate yourself further, listen to feedback, and strive to improve. Over time, these small adjustments will become second nature, helping to create a more respectful and inclusive environment for everyone.

I've had my share of missteps, and each one has been a learning experience. The key is to approach these moments with humility and a genuine desire to do better. It's not about being perfect—it's about being committed to growth.

Navigating Social Interactions for Gender and Sexuality Diverse Individuals

Engaging with Traditional Genders and Sexualities

For individuals from gender and sexuality diverse communities, navigating interactions in environments that may not fully understand or accept gender diversity can be challenging. It's important to assert your identity confidently while also recognizing that others may be at different stages of understanding or acceptance.

When engaging in conversations with those who may hold traditional views on gender and sexuality, consider using clear and direct language to express your identity. You might say, "I use they/them pronouns," or "I'm non-binary." If you encounter misunderstandings or resistance, choose whether to engage in education based on your comfort level. Remember, you are not obligated to educate others, but providing information can sometimes lead to greater understanding.

In my work, I've often counseled individuals on how to navigate these interactions. It's a delicate balance—asserting your identity while also gauging when to educate and when to protect your own well-being. Each situation is unique, and it's important to honor your own comfort levels.

Building Allies and Support Networks

Building a strong support network is crucial for navigating social interactions as a gender and sexuality diverse individual. Allies—

people who actively support and advocate for your rights—can be valuable resources in both personal and professional settings.

Seek out communities and groups that celebrate and support gender and sexual diversity. These spaces provide not only a sense of belonging but also opportunities for mentorship and peer support. Engaging with others who share similar experiences can help you build resilience and confidence in navigating a world that may not always be inclusive.

I've seen the profound impact that a strong support network can have. I've worked with clients who, after finding their community, experienced a newfound sense of empowerment and confidence. These connections remind us that we're not alone, even when the world feels challenging.

Handling Misunderstandings and Discrimination

Unfortunately, misunderstandings and discrimination still occur. When faced with microaggressions or outright discrimination, it's important to prioritize your well-being while also addressing the situation as you see fit.

If you choose to address a microaggression, do so calmly and clearly. For example, if someone makes an insensitive comment, you might respond with, "I understand that wasn't your intention, but that comment can be hurtful because...". In more serious cases of discrimination, consider seeking support from allies, reporting the incident if appropriate, and using available legal resources to protect your rights.

Knowing when to engage and when to protect your mental and emotional health is crucial. There's no obligation to educate others at the cost of your own well-being, and it's perfectly valid to remove yourself from harmful situations.

I've guided many individuals through these tough situations, and one thing remains clear: your well-being comes first. It's okay to step back, seek support, and take care of yourself. The world is slowly changing, and your resilience is part of that change.

Mutual Understanding and Respect in Gender Etiquette

Building Bridges Between Diverse and Traditional Genders and Sexualities

Bridging the gap between diverse and traditional gender identities and sexualities requires open-mindedness and a willingness to engage in meaningful dialogue. Both sides can benefit from understanding each other's perspectives, which can lead to more respectful and empathetic interactions.

When engaging in conversations about gender and sexuality, it's important to approach them with curiosity rather than judgment. Ask questions to learn more about others' experiences and be willing to share your own in a way that fosters mutual respect. Recognizing common ground, such as shared values of respect and dignity, can help facilitate these conversations.

In my career, I've seen how powerful these conversations can be. I remember a client who was initially resistant to discussing gender diversity, but through patient dialogue, they came to see the value in understanding different perspectives. These moments of connection remind me that change is possible, one conversation at a time.

Collaborative Efforts for Inclusivity

Collaboration is key to promoting inclusivity across all gender and sexual identities. This involves working together to create environments where everyone feels valued and respected, regardless of their gender or sexual orientation.

Educational initiatives, advocacy work, and community-building efforts can all contribute to a more inclusive society. By participating in these efforts, whether through formal organizations or informal support networks, individuals from all backgrounds can help foster a culture of inclusivity and respect.

I've had the honor of being part of many collaborative efforts aimed at fostering inclusivity. Whether through workshops, community events, or one-on-one conversations, I've seen how collective action can create lasting change. It's a reminder that we all have a role to play in building a more inclusive world.

Promoting Empathy and Understanding

Empathy is a powerful tool in navigating the complexities of gender and sexual diversity. By making an effort to understand others' experiences and perspectives, we can create more compassionate and inclusive communities.

Storytelling and sharing personal experiences can be particularly effective in fostering empathy. When individuals share their stories, it helps others see beyond labels and stereotypes, leading to a deeper understanding of the diverse experiences that shape our world. Encouraging these conversations in your personal and professional life can contribute to a more empathetic and supportive environment for everyone.

I've always believed in the power of stories. Throughout my life, I've seen how sharing personal experiences—whether my own or those of others—can break down barriers and build connections. It's a practice I encourage in everyone I work with, as it's a key way to promote understanding and empathy.

Practical Tips and Exercises

To help you refine your gender etiquette skills, here are some practical tips and exercises:

1. **Pronoun Practice:** Make a habit of asking for and using pronouns correctly in daily interactions. Practice by role-playing with a friend or using online resources to familiarize yourself with gender-neutral language. Pay attention to how others respond and reflect on how you can improve.

2. **Inclusive Language Audit:** Review your everyday language for gendered terms and practice replacing them with more inclusive alternatives. For example, substitute "guys" with "everyone" or "team." Track your progress over a week and note the impact on your interactions.

3. **Allyship in Action:** Identify opportunities to support gender and sexuality diverse individuals in your community. Attend an LGBTQ+ event, join a diversity committee, or offer support to a friend or colleague. Reflect on how these actions contribute to a more inclusive environment.

4. **Reflection on Experiences:** Reflect on your experiences with gender diversity, considering both positive and challenging interactions. Think about how you can improve your understanding and respect for others' identities. Journal your thoughts and set goals for ongoing learning and improvement.

5. **Educating Others:** If you're comfortable, practice explaining aspects of gender diversity to someone who may not be familiar with the concepts. This could involve sharing an article, having a conversation, or simply answering questions with patience and clarity. Reflect on the experience and consider how you can continue to foster understanding in your circles.

Conclusion: The Ongoing Journey of Gender Etiquette

The Importance of Continuous Learning

Understanding gender etiquette is an ongoing journey that requires continual learning and adaptation. As society evolves, so too do the norms and expectations around gender and sexual diversity. By staying informed and open to learning, you can better navigate these complexities and contribute to a more inclusive and respectful world.

In my years of coaching, I've come to appreciate the importance of humility in this journey. We're all learning, and there's always room for growth. Embracing this mindset has not only enriched my understanding but also deepened my connections with others.

Building a More Inclusive World

Practicing gender etiquette is more than just following social rules—it's about actively contributing to a society where everyone is respected and valued. By fostering understanding, showing respect, and promoting inclusivity, you play a part in building a world that celebrates diversity in all its forms.

I've seen firsthand how even small actions can have a ripple effect. When we choose to respect and include others, we set an example that encourages others to do the same. It's a powerful way to create change, one interaction at a time.

Looking Ahead

As you continue through this guide, you'll explore practical applications of etiquette in specific contexts, such as workplace diversity, social settings, and advocacy for inclusivity. These insights will not only enhance your social and professional life but also empower you to lead with empathy, respect, and understanding in all interactions.

My hope is that, through this journey, you'll find the confidence to navigate the complexities of gender etiquette with grace and kindness. We all have a role to play in making the world a more inclusive place, and by committing to this journey, you're taking an important step in that direction.

SIX

DATING ETIQUETTE

DATING in the modern world can be both exciting and complex, with the rise of online platforms, changing social norms, and evolving expectations around relationships. Whether you're navigating the early stages of dating or building a long-term partnership, understanding and practicing good dating etiquette is essential for creating meaningful connections. Over my 20 years as a relationship coach, I've guided countless individuals through the ups and downs of dating, helping them find balance, respect, and connection in their relationships. This chapter explores the key aspects of modern dating, from making a great first impression to fostering healthy, lasting relationships. We'll also provide practical tips and exercises to help you apply these principles in your dating life.

The Art of Modern Dating

Navigating Online and Offline Dating with Manners

The landscape of dating has expanded significantly with the advent of online platforms, offering new opportunities to connect with potential partners. However, whether you're meeting someone through a dating app or in person, the principles of good manners remain crucial.

- **Online Dating Etiquette:**
- **Profile Honesty:** Your dating profile is often the first impression you make. Ensure it accurately reflects who you are by using recent photos and providing truthful information about your interests, lifestyle, and what you're looking for in a relationship.
- **Respectful Messaging:** When initiating contact online, be respectful and considerate. Avoid generic or overly forward messages, and instead, personalize your approach by referencing something specific from the person's profile. For example, "I noticed you love hiking—I recently explored a great trail near the coast. What's your favorite hiking spot?"
- **Prompt Responses:** If you're interested in someone, respond to messages in a timely manner. If you're not interested, it's polite to let the person know rather than ghosting them. A simple, respectful message such as, "Thank you for your message, but I don't think we're a match. Best of luck!" is appropriate.
- **Offline Dating Etiquette:**
- **Meeting in Person:** When transitioning from online to offline, choose a public place for your first meeting, such as a café or park. This ensures safety and comfort for both parties.
- **Courtesy and Consideration:** Whether online or offline, showing courtesy and consideration is key. Be punctual, listen actively during conversations, and be mindful of the other person's comfort level and boundaries.

Throughout my career, I've seen how the shift to online dating has created new challenges but also new opportunities for connection. I've worked with many clients who initially struggled with the nuances of online communication but eventually found meaningful relationships by applying the same principles of honesty and respect that work in person.

The Importance of Honesty and Clear Communication

Honesty and clear communication are the foundations of any healthy relationship. From the outset, being open about your intentions, feelings, and expectations can prevent misunderstandings and build trust.

- **Setting Expectations:** Early in the dating process, it's important to discuss what you're looking for—whether it's a casual relationship, long-term commitment, or something else. Clear communication helps both parties understand where they stand and whether their goals align.
- **Honesty About Your Life and Past:** While it's natural to want to put your best foot forward, honesty about your life, past experiences, and current circumstances is crucial. Avoid embellishing or hiding significant details that could later affect the relationship.
- **Communicating Boundaries:** Openly discussing boundaries, such as how much time you want to spend together, your comfort levels with physical affection, and personal space, is essential. Respecting these boundaries is just as important as setting them.

I've always emphasized to my clients that the key to a strong relationship is building it on a foundation of truth. I've seen relationships falter when honesty was compromised, and I've also seen the incredible trust and closeness that honesty can create. It's about being true to yourself and giving your partner the same opportunity.

Respecting Boundaries and Personal Space

Respect for boundaries and personal space is critical in any dating scenario. Each person's comfort level is different, and recognizing and honoring these boundaries is a sign of respect and consideration.

- **Physical Boundaries:** Physical boundaries vary widely from person to person. Always seek consent before initiating any form of physical contact, and be attentive to verbal and non-verbal cues that indicate comfort or discomfort.
- **Emotional Boundaries:** Emotional boundaries are just as important. Avoid pressuring your partner to share more than they are comfortable with, and be patient as trust and intimacy develop over time.
- **Personal Space and Time:** Everyone needs personal space and time to themselves. Respect your partner's need for time apart, whether for hobbies, work, or simply to recharge. This respect for individuality helps maintain a healthy balance in the relationship.

One of the most powerful lessons I've learned in my work is the importance of space in relationships. I've seen how giving each other room to breathe and grow can actually bring partners closer together. It's about finding that balance where both people feel valued and respected.

First Date Etiquette

Making a Good First Impression: Attire, Punctuality, and Conversation

The first date sets the tone for any potential relationship, and making a positive impression is key.

- **Attire:** Dressing appropriately for the occasion shows that you care about the date and want to present your best self. Choose an outfit that is neat, comfortable, and suited to the setting—whether it's a casual coffee shop or a formal dinner. Aim to strike a balance between showing your personal style and adhering to the formality of the occasion.
- **Punctuality:** Being on time is a sign of respect for your date's time. Plan ahead to ensure you arrive on time, and if you're

running late due to unforeseen circumstances, communicate promptly with your date.

- **Conversation:** Engage in polite, balanced conversation. Show genuine interest in your date by asking open-ended questions and actively listening to their responses. Avoid dominating the conversation or steering it towards controversial topics like politics or religion, especially on a first date.

I've often reminded clients that the first date isn't just about making an impression—it's about setting the stage for a potential connection. I remember a client who was so nervous about what to wear and say on a first date. After we worked through these concerns, she found that being herself—while also being mindful of these etiquette tips—made the date more enjoyable for both parties.

The Do's and Don'ts of Discussing Personal Topics

Navigating personal topics on a first date can be tricky. While it's important to get to know each other, certain subjects are best approached with caution.

- **Do's:**
- **Light Personal Sharing:** Sharing light personal details, such as your hobbies, interests, and general life experiences, can help build rapport without overwhelming your date.
- **Positive Tone:** Keep the conversation positive and focused on common interests. This helps establish a comfortable and enjoyable atmosphere.
- **Don'ts:**
- **Avoid Over-Sharing:** Refrain from sharing deeply personal or potentially sensitive information, such as past relationship trauma or financial issues, on a first date. These topics are better reserved for when you've built more trust.
- **Stay Clear of Controversial Topics:** Avoid discussing highly charged topics like politics, religion, or deeply personal beliefs, as these can lead to discomfort or conflict early on.

One of the most common mistakes I've seen in dating is rushing into deep or controversial topics too soon. There's a time and place for everything, and first dates are best when they're light and enjoyable. Over time, as trust builds, those deeper conversations can naturally unfold.

Handling the Bill: Splitting, Treating, or Taking Turns

Handling the bill can sometimes be a point of uncertainty on a first date. The key is to approach it with openness and consideration for the other person's comfort.

- **Discussing Payment:** Before the bill arrives, it's helpful to have a brief discussion about how to handle payment. For example, you might say, "How do you usually like to handle the bill?" This opens up a dialogue and sets the stage for mutual agreement.
- **Splitting the Bill:** Splitting the bill is becoming increasingly common and is often the fairest approach, especially on a first date. It signals that both parties are equals and share responsibility for the outing.
- **Offering to Treat:** If one person offers to treat the other, it's polite to express appreciation. However, be mindful not to assume that this will always be the case in future dates. Taking turns treating each other on subsequent dates can be a balanced approach.
- **Accepting or Declining Offers:** If your date insists on paying and you're comfortable with it, graciously accept the gesture. If you prefer to split or contribute, express your preference kindly but be willing to accept their offer if they insist.

I've often told clients that how you handle the bill says a lot about your values and your approach to relationships. It's not about the money—it's about communication, respect, and setting the tone for mutual understanding from the very beginning.

Communication and Conflict Resolution in Dating

Effective communication is the cornerstone of a healthy relationship, and this includes both positive interactions and conflict resolution.

- **Open and Honest Dialogue:** From the early stages of dating, cultivate an environment where both partners feel comfortable expressing their thoughts, feelings, and concerns. Regularly check in with each other to ensure that both partners' needs are being met.
- **Conflict Resolution:** Disagreements are inevitable in any relationship. When conflicts arise, address them calmly and constructively. Focus on the issue at hand rather than attacking the other person, and work together to find a solution. For example, use "I" statements to express how you feel, such as "I felt hurt when..." instead of "You made me feel...".
- **Active Listening:** During discussions, especially during conflicts, practice active listening. This means fully concentrating on what your partner is saying, acknowledging their feelings, and responding thoughtfully.

In my practice, I've seen how crucial communication is to the health of a relationship. I've worked with couples who learned to communicate effectively and saw their relationship transform as a result. It's about creating a space where both partners feel heard and valued.

Respecting Individuality and Personal Growth

A healthy relationship is one where both partners support each other's individuality and personal growth.

- **Encouraging Independence:** Encourage your partner to pursue their interests, hobbies, and goals. Independence is important for maintaining a balanced and fulfilling relationship.

- **Supporting Growth:** Celebrate your partner's achievements and support their efforts to grow, whether it's in their career, personal development, or other pursuits. A relationship should be a source of mutual encouragement and motivation.
- **Balancing Togetherness and Space:** Striking a balance between spending quality time together and allowing space for individual pursuits is key. Respect your partner's need for alone time or time with friends and family, just as you would expect them to respect yours.

I've always believed that a strong relationship is built on the foundation of two whole individuals coming together. I've seen relationships thrive when both partners encourage each other's growth and respect each other's need for space.

The Role of Etiquette in Long-Term Relationships

Etiquette plays a significant role not just in the early stages of dating but throughout long-term relationships as well.

- **Consistent Respect and Kindness:** In a long-term relationship, it's easy to take your partner for granted. However, maintaining the same level of respect, kindness, and consideration as you did in the beginning is crucial for the relationship's longevity. Small gestures of appreciation, such as saying "thank you," complimenting your partner, or surprising them with a thoughtful act, can keep the relationship strong.
- **Shared Responsibilities:** In long-term relationships, sharing responsibilities fairly is essential. Whether it's household chores, financial decisions, or emotional labor, ensure that both partners feel that their contributions are valued and balanced.
- **Continual Communication:** As the relationship evolves, so

do the needs and dynamics of both partners. Continually communicate with each other about your needs, goals, and any changes in the relationship. This ongoing dialogue helps to prevent misunderstandings and fosters a deeper connection.

Over the years, I've seen how small acts of kindness and ongoing communication can keep a relationship vibrant and fulfilling. It's about continuing to invest in the relationship, even as it matures, to ensure that both partners feel loved and appreciated.

Practical Tips and Exercises

To help you refine your dating etiquette, here are some practical tips and exercises:

1. **Online Profile Audit:** Review your online dating profile to ensure it accurately reflects who you are. Update your photos, rewrite your bio to be both honest and engaging, and check for any inconsistencies that might give a misleading impression.
2. **Practice Boundary Setting:** Reflect on your personal boundaries—both physical and emotional—and practice communicating them clearly in hypothetical dating scenarios. This might include role-playing with a friend or journaling about how you would handle certain situations.
3. **First Date Role-Play:** Practice a first-date scenario with a friend. Focus on making a good first impression by discussing appropriate topics, handling the bill, and ensuring a balanced conversation. Afterward, ask for feedback on how you came across and what you can improve.
4. **Conflict Resolution Reflection:** Think about a recent disagreement or conflict you've had in a relationship (romantic or otherwise). Reflect on how you handled it and

consider how you could apply the conflict resolution techniques discussed in this chapter to future situations.

5. **Gratitude Practice:** In an existing relationship, take time each day to express gratitude to your partner for something they've done, no matter how small. This could be through a compliment, a thank you, or a small gesture. Notice how this practice affects the dynamics of your relationship.

Conclusion: The Journey of Dating Etiquette

The Importance of Continued Learning

Dating etiquette is not a one-time lesson but an ongoing journey that evolves with your experiences and relationships. As you navigate the complexities of modern dating, continue to learn and adapt your approach to ensure that your interactions are respectful, meaningful, and considerate.

In my years of coaching, I've learned that dating, like any relationship, is a journey of growth. It's about being open to learning, willing to adapt, and committed to treating others with kindness and respect. This mindset not only improves your dating experiences but also enriches your life.

Building Lasting Connections

The principles of good dating etiquette—honesty, respect, clear communication, and mutual support—are the foundation of lasting relationships. Whether you're at the beginning of your dating journey or deepening a long-term partnership, these values will help you build strong, healthy connections.

I've had the privilege of watching many clients find love and build strong, lasting relationships by applying these principles. It's a reminder that good etiquette isn't just about rules—it's about building connections that stand the test of time.

Looking Ahead

As you continue through this guide, you'll explore further aspects of modern etiquette, including how to navigate complex social settings and promote inclusivity in all areas of life. These skills will not only enhance your dating experiences but also empower you to engage with others in a way that fosters respect, understanding, and genuine connection.

The journey of dating etiquette is one of continuous learning and growth. I encourage you to embrace each experience as an opportunity to refine your approach, deepen your connections, and build a relationship that is rooted in mutual respect and love.

SEVEN

WEDDING ETIQUETTE

WEDDINGS ARE a celebration of love and commitment, but they are also complex social events that involve careful planning, cultural considerations, and the navigation of relationships. Whether you are the couple getting married, a guest, or part of the wedding party, understanding the nuances of wedding etiquette is essential for ensuring that the day runs smoothly and is enjoyable for everyone involved. Over the years, as both a bride and a frequent wedding guest, I've experienced the joy and challenges that come with weddings. Additionally, in my work as a relationship coach, I've helped countless couples navigate the intricacies of planning and participating in their special day. This chapter provides a comprehensive guide to wedding etiquette, covering everything from the couple's responsibilities to guest behavior and the roles of the wedding party. Practical tips and exercises are included to help you prepare for and participate in weddings with grace and confidence.

The Couple's Guide to Wedding Etiquette

Announcements and Invitations: Wording and Timing

The first step in planning a wedding is announcing your engagement and sending out invitations. Both of these elements are important as they set the tone for your wedding and help communicate your plans to your loved ones.

- **Engagement Announcements:** Traditionally, couples announce their engagement to close family and friends before making a public announcement. This can be done in person, over the phone, or through a video call. Once the immediate family is informed, the couple can announce the engagement more broadly, often through social media or a formal announcement in a local newspaper.
- **Save-the-Date Cards:** Save-the-date cards are typically sent out six to eight months before the wedding. These cards provide basic information about the wedding date and location, allowing guests to plan ahead. While not mandatory, they are particularly useful for destination weddings or when many guests will be traveling from afar.
- **Wedding Invitations:** Invitations should be sent out six to eight weeks before the wedding. The wording of the invitation should reflect the formality of the event. For example, a formal wedding might use traditional phrasing such as, "The honor of your presence is requested," while a more casual event might say, "Please join us to celebrate." Be sure to include all necessary details, such as the time, date, location, dress code, and RSVP instructions.

When I got married, one of the most joyful moments was announcing our engagement to our families. But as a coach, I've also seen how important it is to be clear and considerate with invitations —making sure that everyone feels included and informed from the start.

Navigating Guest Lists and Seating Arrangements

Creating a guest list and arranging seating can be one of the most challenging aspects of wedding planning. It requires balancing your desires with those of your families, as well as logistical considerations.

- **Guest List:** Start by making a preliminary list of everyone you'd like to invite, then refine it based on your budget and venue capacity. It's important to be consistent with how you allocate invitations—for example, if you're inviting some cousins, it's courteous to invite all of them. If you're dealing with limited space, consider prioritizing close family and friends.
- **Seating Arrangements:** The seating arrangement is often determined by the formality of the event. For formal weddings, a seating chart is usually provided, while more casual weddings may allow for open seating. When creating a seating chart, consider relationships and group dynamics. Try to seat people with others they know and get along with, and avoid placing anyone in a situation that might cause discomfort. Additionally, consider placing older guests or those with mobility issues closer to exits or restrooms for their convenience.

I recall the careful consideration my husband and I put into our guest list—wanting to include everyone we cared about, while also navigating the tricky waters of family dynamics. It was a balancing act, but one that paid off in the end, as everyone felt welcomed and valued.

Managing Family Dynamics and Traditions

Weddings often bring together different family traditions and dynamics, which can sometimes lead to tension. Handling these situations with sensitivity and respect is key to ensuring a harmonious celebration.

- **Blending Traditions:** If you and your partner come from different cultural or religious backgrounds, discuss which traditions are important to each of you and how they can be incorporated into your wedding. This might involve having multiple ceremonies, combining elements from each tradition, or finding new ways to honor both families.

- **Dealing with Family Expectations:** Family members often have strong opinions about weddings, especially if they are contributing financially. While it's important to respect their wishes, remember that this is your wedding, and you should feel comfortable making decisions that reflect your values and preferences. Communicate openly with your family about your plans and be prepared to compromise where necessary.

- **Handling Sensitive Relationships:** Weddings can sometimes bring unresolved family issues to the surface. If you anticipate tension between certain guests, consider seating arrangements or other strategies to minimize conflict. It may also be helpful to have a trusted friend or family member act as a mediator on the day of the wedding.

As a coach, I've often worked with couples facing the challenge of blending traditions and managing family expectations. It's not always easy, but with open communication and a willingness to compromise, it's possible to create a day that honors both your backgrounds and your future together.

Guest Etiquette at Weddings

RSVP Etiquette and Gift-Giving Guidelines

As a wedding guest, your primary responsibilities are to respond to the invitation in a timely manner and to select an appropriate gift for the couple.

- **RSVP Etiquette:** Responding to a wedding invitation as soon as possible is a matter of courtesy and helps the couple with their planning. Follow the RSVP instructions provided— whether it's through a card, email, or website. If you must decline, do so politely and offer your best wishes to the couple.

- **Selecting a Gift:** Wedding gifts are a traditional way to celebrate the couple's union. If the couple has a registry, selecting a gift from it ensures that you are giving something they truly want or need. If there is no registry, consider giving a gift that reflects the couple's tastes or a contribution towards their future, such as a cash gift or a donation to a charity in their name.
- **Navigating Modern and Inter-Cultural Gift-Giving Behaviors:**
- **Wishing Wells and Cash Gifts:** Many couples today prefer cash gifts, especially if they already have a fully equipped home. If the invitation mentions a wishing well or cash gifts, this is a clear indication of the couple's preference. However, if you're uncomfortable giving cash, it's perfectly acceptable to choose a meaningful gift instead.
- **Cultural Considerations:** In some cultures, specific types of gifts are traditional, such as money in a red envelope in Chinese weddings. If you're attending a wedding from a culture different from your own, it's respectful to familiarize yourself with these traditions and participate appropriately.

I've attended weddings where the gift-giving etiquette was very different from what I was accustomed to, and I've learned that respecting cultural practices can deepen the experience and show the couple that you honor their traditions.

Appropriate Attire for Different Types of Weddings

Choosing the right attire for a wedding is important, as it shows respect for the couple and the formality of the event. The invitation will often provide clues about the dress code.

- **Formal/Black Tie:** For a black-tie wedding, men should wear a tuxedo, while women should opt for a formal evening gown. Accessories should be elegant and understated.

- **Semi-Formal/Black Tie Optional:** A semi-formal or black-tie optional wedding allows for more flexibility. Men can wear a dark suit and tie, while women can choose a cocktail dress or a dressy suit.
- **Casual:** Casual weddings typically take place during the day or in informal settings. Men can wear slacks with a button-down shirt or a blazer, while women might choose a sundress or a skirt and blouse. However, even for a casual wedding, avoid overly casual items like jeans, shorts, or flip-flops unless explicitly stated as acceptable.
- **Cultural or Themed Weddings:** If the wedding has a specific cultural or thematic dress code, do your best to adhere to it. For example, if it's a traditional Indian wedding, wearing a sari or a kurta would be appropriate. If you're unsure about the dress code, it's always a good idea to ask the couple or the wedding planner for guidance.

I still remember attending a wedding that required formal attire, and how special it felt to dress up and participate in such a significant day. Paying attention to the dress code not only respects the couple's wishes but also enhances the overall experience for everyone involved.

How to Behave at the Ceremony and Reception

Your behavior at both the ceremony and reception reflects your respect for the couple and the significance of their wedding day.

- **Arriving on Time:** Arriving on time is crucial, especially for the ceremony. Plan to arrive at least 15 minutes early to ensure you're seated before the event begins. If you do arrive late, wait for an appropriate moment, such as between readings or during a musical interlude, to quietly find a seat.
- **Participating Respectfully:** During the ceremony, follow the lead of the officiant and the couple. If you're unsure whether to stand, sit, or participate in a specific ritual, observe those around you and act accordingly. If the ceremony includes

religious or cultural practices that are unfamiliar to you, participate respectfully, or simply observe if you're uncomfortable participating.

- **Interacting at the Reception:** At the reception, engage with other guests, congratulate the couple, and participate in any activities, such as toasts or dancing, as appropriate. However, be mindful of your alcohol consumption, and avoid behaviors that could disrupt the event. The focus should always remain on celebrating the couple's union.

As a guest, I've always found that the key to enjoying a wedding is to fully engage in the experience—whether it's the quiet reverence of the ceremony or the joyful celebration at the reception. It's a day for making memories, and your respectful participation is part of what makes it special for the couple.

The Role of the Wedding Party

Responsibilities and Expectations for Bridesmaids and Groomsmen

As a member of the wedding party, you play a significant role in supporting the couple and helping to ensure their wedding day is memorable and stress-free.

- **Pre-Wedding Support:** Bridesmaids and groomsmen often assist with planning and organizing pre-wedding events, such as bridal showers, bachelor/bachelorette parties, and rehearsal dinners. This may also involve helping with tasks like addressing invitations, running errands, or offering emotional support.
- **Attire and Presentation:** The couple will typically choose the attire for the wedding party. It's your responsibility to ensure your outfit is tailored and ready for the big day. On the wedding day, arrive early and be prepared to assist with any last-minute preparations or issues.

- **Ceremony Participation:** During the ceremony, the wedding party typically has specific roles, such as walking down the aisle, holding rings, or standing alongside the couple. It's important to understand your role and practice any movements or lines during the rehearsal.
- **Financial Considerations:** Being part of the wedding party can involve expenses, such as purchasing attire, contributing to pre-wedding events, and travel. Discuss these expectations with the couple early on to avoid any misunderstandings.

Having been a bridesmaid several times, I know firsthand the level of commitment and responsibility that comes with the role. But I also know how rewarding it is to stand by a friend or family member on one of the most important days of their life.

Hosting and Attending Pre-Wedding Events

The wedding party often hosts or helps plan pre-wedding events, which are important opportunities to celebrate the couple and help them prepare for their big day.

- **Bridal Showers and Bachelor/Bachelorette Parties:** These events should reflect the couple's personalities and preferences. When planning, consider what the couple would enjoy most—whether it's a lively night out, a relaxing spa day, or a themed party. Always keep the couple's comfort and wishes in mind, and ensure that the events are inclusive and enjoyable for all guests.
- **Rehearsal Dinner:** The rehearsal dinner is typically held the night before the wedding and includes the couple, the wedding party, and close family members. It's often hosted by the groom's family, but this can vary. As part of the wedding party, your role may involve assisting with last-minute details or simply attending to show your support.

I've found that pre-wedding events are often where some of the best memories are made. Whether it's a relaxed gathering or a more elaborate celebration, these moments help build anticipation for the big day and bring everyone closer together.

Supporting the Couple Throughout the Wedding Process

Your support as a member of the wedding party extends beyond the day of the wedding. From the engagement to the honeymoon, your role is to help the couple navigate this significant life event.

- **Emotional Support:** Weddings can be stressful, and the couple may need emotional support throughout the planning process. Be available to listen, offer advice if asked, and help alleviate any anxieties they may have.
- **Practical Assistance:** On the wedding day, be prepared to assist with any tasks that arise, whether it's helping the bride or groom get dressed, coordinating with vendors, or managing logistics. Your proactive involvement can help ensure everything runs smoothly.
- **Post-Wedding Support:** After the wedding, the couple may appreciate help with tasks such as returning rentals, distributing thank-you notes, or even assisting with post-wedding gatherings. Continue to offer your support as they transition into married life.

I've always encouraged the wedding party to think of themselves as the couple's support system. It's about more than just standing at the altar—it's about being there for them every step of the way, making their journey into marriage as smooth and joyful as possible.

Practical Tips and Exercises

To help you refine your wedding etiquette skills, here are some practical tips and exercises:

1. **Draft a Wedding Invitation:** Practice drafting a wedding invitation that reflects the tone and formality of your (or a

hypothetical) wedding. Pay attention to the wording, ensuring it's clear, respectful, and inclusive.

2. **RSVP Role-Play:** With a friend, role-play responding to a wedding invitation. Practice polite acceptance and polite declines, and discuss what you would do if circumstances changed after you had already RSVPed.

3. **Gift Selection Exercise:** Research wedding gift registries and practice selecting a gift that balances practicality with personal sentiment. If the couple prefers cash gifts, consider how you would present this in a thoughtful and respectful manner.

4. **Attire Planning:** Review different wedding dress codes and plan an appropriate outfit for each scenario. Consider how you would adapt your attire for a cultural or themed wedding and discuss your choices with a friend or family member for feedback.

5. **Pre-Wedding Event Planning:** If you're part of a wedding party, brainstorm ideas for a bridal shower, bachelor/bachelorette party, or rehearsal dinner that aligns with the couple's interests and preferences. Consider logistics, guest lists, and activities that would make the event special.

Conclusion: The Timeless Importance of Wedding Etiquette

The Role of Etiquette in Creating Memorable Celebrations

Weddings are once-in-a-lifetime events that bring together family, friends, and loved ones to celebrate a union. The role of etiquette in these events cannot be understated—it helps to create an atmosphere of respect, joy, and harmony that ensures the day is as memorable as possible for everyone involved.

As I've seen in my own life and work, the magic of a wedding often lies in the details—how we treat each other, how we honor traditions, and how we come together to celebrate love. Etiquette is what helps us navigate these moments with grace and thoughtfulness.

The Ongoing Journey of Etiquette

Whether you're the couple getting married, a guest, or a member of the wedding party, the principles of wedding etiquette—respect, consideration, and thoughtfulness—extend beyond the wedding day. They are the foundation of all social interactions, helping to build and maintain meaningful relationships.

I've learned that the lessons we take from weddings—about respect, kindness, and connection—apply to so many other areas of life. Weddings may be special occasions, but the etiquette we practice there enriches all our relationships.

Looking Ahead

As you continue through this guide, you'll explore further aspects of modern etiquette, including navigating complex social settings, workplace dynamics, and promoting inclusivity in all areas of life. These skills will not only enhance your experience at weddings but also empower you to engage with others in a way that fosters respect, understanding, and genuine connection in every aspect of your life.

The journey of mastering etiquette is ongoing, and as you learn and grow, you'll find that these principles will serve you well in every corner of your life—at weddings and beyond.

EIGHT

ETIQUETTE AROUND MARGINALIZED COMMUNITIES

UNDERSTANDING AND PRACTICING inclusivity is an essential aspect of modern etiquette. Interacting with marginalized communities—whether based on race, ethnicity, disability, gender, sexual orientation, or other factors—requires sensitivity, respect, and a commitment to recognizing and addressing the challenges these communities face. As someone who is neurodivergent, a parent to two neurodivergent children, and a friend to many people with disabilities, I have seen firsthand the importance of fostering environments where everyone feels respected and valued. In my work as a relationship coach, I've had the privilege of helping people from marginalized communities navigate social and professional challenges, and it's from these experiences that I share the following insights. This chapter provides guidance on how to engage with marginalized communities with empathy and understanding, while also offering practical advice on being an effective ally. Through exploring these topics, we aim to foster a deeper understanding of inclusivity and provide actionable steps to promote a more inclusive society.

The Importance of Respect and Consideration for All Individuals

At the core of all etiquette is the principle of respect—recognizing the inherent dignity and worth of every individual. This respect extends to all people, regardless of their background, identity, or abilities. Modern etiquette demands that we go beyond mere politeness and actively work to ensure that everyone feels valued and included in social and professional settings.

Respecting others means acknowledging their unique experiences and challenges. It involves being mindful of how our words and actions affect those around us and striving to create environments where everyone feels welcome. This respect should be the foundation of all interactions, guiding our behavior toward those from marginalized communities.

Reflecting on my own experiences, I remember moments when, as a neurodivergent person, I felt out of place or misunderstood in social situations. It wasn't always because people were intentionally unkind; often, it was simply a lack of awareness. This is why respect and consideration are so crucial—they help bridge gaps in understanding and make everyone feel included.

Recognizing and Addressing Unconscious Bias

Unconscious bias refers to the attitudes or stereotypes that affect our understanding, actions, and decisions in an unconscious manner. These biases are often deeply ingrained and can influence how we interact with others, sometimes leading to unintentional discrimination or exclusion.

Recognizing unconscious bias is the first step in addressing it. This requires self-reflection and a willingness to challenge our own assumptions. Ask yourself questions like: "Do I treat people differently based on their appearance or background?" or "Am I making assumptions about someone's abilities or intentions without getting to know them?"

Addressing unconscious bias involves actively working to counteract these tendencies. This might include seeking out diverse perspectives, educating yourself about different cultures and identities, and making a conscious effort to treat everyone with the same level of respect and consideration.

As someone who has worked closely with marginalized communities, I've had to confront my own biases and assumptions. It's a continuous journey, one that requires humility and a commitment to growth. By challenging our biases, we can create more inclusive and supportive environments for everyone.

The Role of Empathy in Interactions with Marginalized Communities

Empathy is the ability to understand and share the feelings of another person. In the context of interacting with marginalized communities, empathy involves recognizing the unique challenges these communities face and responding with kindness, support, and understanding.

Empathy requires listening without judgment, being open to learning from others' experiences, and offering support in ways that are meaningful and respectful. It's about putting yourself in someone else's shoes and considering how your actions and words might impact them. By cultivating empathy, we can build stronger, more inclusive relationships and contribute to a more just and equitable society.

As a parent of neurodivergent children, I've seen how empathy can make a world of difference. When teachers, friends, and even strangers approach my children with empathy, they help create an environment where my kids feel understood and supported. This is the kind of impact we can all have when we lead with empathy.

Engaging with Minority Communities

Cultural Sensitivity and Respect for Diverse Backgrounds

Cultural sensitivity is an essential aspect of engaging with minority communities. It involves recognizing and respecting the diverse cultural practices, beliefs, and values that exist within these communities. This sensitivity is crucial in both social and professional settings.

- **Learn and Educate Yourself:** Take the time to learn about the cultural backgrounds of those you interact with. This might involve reading books, attending cultural events, or simply asking respectful questions. Educating yourself shows that you value and respect their culture.
- **Respect Cultural Practices:** When engaging with someone from a different cultural background, be mindful of their practices and customs. For example, some cultures have specific norms around greetings, personal space, or dress codes. Respecting these practices is a key part of cultural sensitivity.
- **Avoiding Cultural Appropriation:** Cultural appropriation occurs when elements of a minority culture are adopted by members of a dominant culture in a way that is disrespectful or exploitative. Be mindful of how you engage with aspects of other cultures and ensure that your actions are rooted in respect and understanding.

In my work with clients from diverse cultural backgrounds, I've learned the importance of cultural sensitivity. It's not just about avoiding offense—it's about showing genuine respect for the rich tapestry of experiences and traditions that make up our world. This respect fosters trust and strengthens relationships.

Avoiding Stereotypes and Generalizations

Stereotypes and generalizations are harmful because they reduce individuals to simplistic and often inaccurate labels based on their identity. Avoiding stereotypes is crucial for building respectful and meaningful relationships with people from minority communities.

- **See the Individual:** Treat each person as an individual rather than a representative of their group. Recognize that people within any community are diverse and have their own unique experiences, perspectives, and identities.
- **Challenge Assumptions:** If you find yourself making assumptions based on someone's race, ethnicity, gender, or other characteristics, take a moment to question where these assumptions come from and whether they are fair or accurate.
- **Listen and Learn:** Instead of relying on stereotypes, take the time to listen to people's stories and learn about their experiences firsthand. This not only fosters understanding but also helps to break down harmful stereotypes.

I've often encountered stereotypes about neurodivergence, both in my own life and in my work with clients. These assumptions can be incredibly limiting and hurtful. By seeing each person as an individual, we can move beyond stereotypes and build more authentic connections.

Supporting Inclusivity in Social and Professional Settings

Creating inclusive environments in both social and professional settings requires intentional effort and a commitment to fairness and equality.

- **Inclusive Language:** Use language that is inclusive and respectful. This includes using correct pronouns, avoiding gendered language when unnecessary, and being mindful of terms that might be offensive or outdated.
- **Inclusive Practices:** In professional settings, ensure that policies and practices are inclusive of all employees. This might involve providing accommodations for people with disabilities, offering diversity training, and ensuring equal opportunities for all.
- **Inclusive Events:** When organizing social or professional events, consider how you can make them accessible and

welcoming to everyone. This might include providing dietary options for different cultural practices, ensuring physical accessibility, or scheduling events at times that accommodate diverse needs.

In my coaching practice, I've seen how inclusive language and practices can transform environments. It's about making sure that everyone feels they belong, and that their unique contributions are valued. This approach not only benefits marginalized communities but enriches the entire group.

Etiquette for Interacting with People with Disabilities

Understanding Visible and Invisible Disabilities

Disabilities can be visible or invisible, and it's important to recognize that people with disabilities face unique challenges that may not always be apparent to others.

- **Visible Disabilities:** These include physical disabilities that are easily noticeable, such as the use of a wheelchair, cane, or hearing aid. When interacting with someone with a visible disability, it's important to be respectful and considerate, without making assumptions about their abilities or limitations.
- **Invisible Disabilities:** These include conditions that are not immediately apparent, such as chronic pain, mental health conditions, or neurodivergence. It's important to recognize that just because a disability isn't visible doesn't mean it's not real or impactful. Be mindful that someone's behavior or needs might be influenced by an invisible disability.

As a neurodivergent person and a mother to neurodivergent children, I've learned firsthand the importance of recognizing invisible disabilities. Just because someone's challenges aren't visible doesn't mean they aren't there. Understanding this can help us all be more compassionate and supportive.

Appropriate Language and Behavior in Interactions

Using appropriate language and behavior when interacting with people with disabilities is crucial for fostering respectful and positive interactions.

- **Use Person-First Language:** Person-first language puts the person before their disability (e.g., "person with a disability" rather than "disabled person"). This emphasizes their identity as an individual rather than defining them by their disability. However, it's important to recognize that some people prefer identity-first language (e.g., "disabled person"). When in doubt, ask the individual what they prefer.
- **Offer Assistance, Don't Assume:** If you think someone might need help, it's polite to offer assistance, but don't assume they need it. Ask, "Would you like any help?" and respect their response. Never force help on someone if they decline.
- **Respect Personal Space:** For individuals using mobility aids, such as wheelchairs or canes, these devices are part of their personal space. Avoid touching or leaning on them without permission. Similarly, when communicating with someone who is Deaf or hard of hearing, ensure you're facing them directly, as they may rely on lip-reading or facial expressions.

Through my interactions with friends and family members who have disabilities, I've learned the importance of asking rather than assuming. This simple act of respect goes a long way in making others feel valued and respected.

Creating Inclusive Environments for People with Physical Disabilities and Neurodivergence

Creating inclusive environments involves making spaces and activities accessible to everyone, regardless of their abilities.

- **Physical Accessibility:** Ensure that physical spaces are accessible to people with disabilities. This might involve providing ramps, elevators, and accessible restrooms, as well as ensuring that seating arrangements accommodate wheelchairs and other mobility aids.
- **Sensory Considerations:** For individuals with sensory sensitivities, such as those on the autism spectrum, consider how environments can be adapted to reduce sensory overload. This might involve providing quiet spaces, reducing harsh lighting, or offering noise-canceling options.
- **Inclusive Communication:** For individuals with neurodivergence, such as autism or ADHD, clear and direct communication is often appreciated. Avoid using overly complex language or abstract concepts, and be patient if someone needs extra time to process information or respond.

In my home, we've made adaptations to ensure that my neurodivergent children feel comfortable and supported. These small changes, like creating quiet spaces and using clear communication, have made a significant difference in their well-being. These are lessons I carry into my professional life as well, helping others create environments that are truly inclusive.

Supporting Inclusivity and Allyship

How to Be an Ally to Marginalized Communities

Being an ally involves actively supporting and advocating for marginalized communities. This means not only recognizing the challenges these communities face but also taking concrete steps to help address them.

- **Educate Yourself:** An effective ally is informed. Take the time to learn about the history, struggles, and achievements of marginalized communities. This knowledge will help you understand the context of the challenges they face and how you can best support them.

- **Speak Up:** When you witness discrimination or exclusion, speak up. Whether it's calling out a harmful joke, challenging unfair practices, or standing up for someone who is being marginalized, your voice can make a difference.
- **Support Marginalized Voices:** Amplify the voices of those from marginalized communities by sharing their stories, supporting their work, and advocating for their inclusion. This might involve promoting their businesses, attending their events, or simply listening and learning from their experiences.

In my career, I've seen the power of allyship. Whether it's supporting a friend with a disability or advocating for inclusive policies at work, being an ally is about action as much as it is about intention. It's about making a real difference in the lives of those who need it most.

Navigating Conversations About Identity and Inclusion

Conversations about identity and inclusion can be sensitive, but they are essential for fostering understanding and promoting inclusivity.

- **Approach with Humility:** When discussing issues of identity and inclusion, approach the conversation with humility and a willingness to learn. Recognize that you may not have all the answers and be open to hearing different perspectives.
- **Listen Actively:** Active listening involves fully engaging with what the other person is saying, without interrupting or immediately forming a response. This shows respect for their experiences and helps build trust.
- **Be Open to Feedback:** If someone from a marginalized community offers feedback on your behavior or language, receive it with gratitude rather than defensiveness. This feedback is a valuable opportunity to learn and grow.

As a coach, I've often facilitated difficult conversations about identity and inclusion. I've learned that approaching these discussions with an open heart and a willingness to listen can lead to profound understanding and change. It's not always easy, but it's always worth it.

Promoting Diversity and Inclusion in Everyday Life

Promoting diversity and inclusion isn't limited to specific events or conversations—it's something that should be woven into the fabric of your everyday life.

- **Inclusive Decision-Making:** In both your personal and professional life, consider how your decisions impact marginalized communities. This might involve supporting diverse businesses, advocating for inclusive policies, or ensuring that everyone has a voice in group decisions.
- **Challenge Exclusionary Practices:** When you encounter practices or policies that exclude certain groups, challenge them. This could involve speaking up in meetings, advocating for change, or simply modeling inclusive behavior.
- **Celebrate Diversity:** Make an effort to celebrate diversity in all its forms. This might involve attending cultural events, learning about different traditions, or simply appreciating the richness that diversity brings to your community.

In my work and personal life, I've seen how small, everyday actions can have a big impact. Whether it's choosing to support a minority-owned business or advocating for more inclusive practices at work, these decisions add up. They create a world where everyone has a place, where everyone is seen and valued.

Practical Tips and Exercises

To help you refine your etiquette around marginalized communities, here are some practical tips and exercises:

1. **Unconscious Bias Reflection:** Take a moment to reflect on your own unconscious biases. Consider situations where you may have made assumptions about someone based on their identity. How can you work to challenge these biases in the future?

2. **Cultural Sensitivity Exercise:** Choose a culture that you are less familiar with and spend time learning about its customs, traditions, and values. Reflect on how you can incorporate this knowledge into your interactions with people from that culture.

3. **Accessibility Audit:** Review a space you frequently use (your home, workplace, or a community venue) for accessibility. Consider how it could be made more inclusive for people with disabilities and what changes could be implemented to improve accessibility.

4. **Active Listening Practice:** Engage in a conversation about identity or inclusion with someone from a marginalized community. Practice active listening, focusing on understanding their perspective without interrupting or offering immediate responses. Reflect on what you learned from the conversation.

5. **Allyship in Action:** Identify a situation where you can actively support a marginalized community. This might involve attending a protest, supporting a minority-owned business, or advocating for inclusive policies in your workplace. Reflect on how these actions contribute to promoting inclusivity.

Conclusion: The Essential Role of Inclusivity in Modern Etiquette

Inclusivity as the Foundation of Respectful Interactions

Inclusivity is at the heart of modern etiquette, guiding how we interact with others and ensuring that everyone is treated with dignity and respect. By understanding and practicing inclusivity, we can create environments where all individuals feel valued and included.

Reflecting on my own experiences, both personal and professional, I've seen how inclusivity transforms lives. It's more than just a practice—it's a commitment to seeing and valuing every person for who they are.

The Ongoing Journey of Learning and Growth

Understanding and supporting marginalized communities is an ongoing journey that requires continuous learning, reflection, and action. As society evolves, so too must our approach to inclusivity, ensuring that we are always striving to create a more just and equitable world.

For me, this journey is deeply personal. As a neurodivergent person and the parent of neurodivergent children, I've seen the power of inclusivity firsthand. It's a journey I'm committed to, and one I encourage everyone to undertake.

Looking Ahead

As you continue through this guide, you'll explore further aspects of modern etiquette, including how to navigate complex social settings and workplace dynamics, and how to foster inclusive environments in all areas of life. These skills will not only enhance your interactions with marginalized communities but also empower you to be a force for positive change in your community and beyond.

The journey of understanding and practicing inclusivity is ongoing, but it's one that enriches our lives and the lives of those around us. Together, we can create a world where everyone feels respected, valued, and included.

NINE

DINING ETIQUETTE

DINING ETIQUETTE IS MORE than a set of rules—it's a way of showing respect and consideration for others, making meals enjoyable, and navigating diverse cultural contexts with grace. Whether you're dining in a formal setting, attending a casual gathering, or hosting a meal, understanding and practicing good dining etiquette is essential. Throughout my career as a relationship coach and in my personal life, I've seen how dining can bring people together, foster connections, and create lasting memories. This chapter explores various aspects of dining etiquette, from cultural considerations to formal and casual dining, providing you with the tools to dine with style and confidence.

Cultural Considerations in Dining Etiquette

Dining Etiquette Across Cultures

Dining etiquette varies widely across cultures, and understanding these differences is essential when dining in international or multi-cultural settings. Being aware of cultural norms and customs can help you avoid unintentional faux pas and demonstrate respect for the traditions of others.

- **Cultural Norms Around Food:** Different cultures have unique customs surrounding food, including how it's prepared, served, and consumed. For example, in Japan, it's customary to eat sushi with your hands or chopsticks, and slurping noodles is considered a sign of appreciation. In contrast, in many Western cultures, slurping is seen as impolite. My travels and work have shown me how these small gestures can significantly impact the dining experience and the connections we form with others.
- **Use of Utensils:** The use of utensils also differs across cultures. In some cultures, such as in India or parts of the Middle East, eating with your hands is common and expected, while in Western cultures, using a knife, fork, and spoon is standard. Understanding these differences allows you to adapt to various dining environments with ease.
- **Seating Arrangements and Hierarchy:** In many cultures, seating arrangements at the dining table reflect social hierarchy. For instance, in Chinese dining, the seat facing the entrance is often reserved for the host or the most honored guest. Knowing where to sit and how to show respect to elders or guests of honor is important in such contexts. During a dinner I once attended in China, I learned how deeply these customs are valued, and how observing them can build trust and mutual respect.
- **Religious and Dietary Considerations:** Be aware of religious and dietary restrictions that may affect what people can eat. For instance, Muslims may avoid pork and require halal food, while Jews may observe kosher dietary laws. Vegetarians and vegans also have specific dietary needs. Understanding and respecting these restrictions is crucial when dining with others from diverse backgrounds. As someone who often hosts dinners, I've found that asking about dietary preferences ahead of time not only shows respect but also creates a more inclusive and enjoyable experience for all.

Navigating Formal Dining Settings

Formal dining occasions, such as banquets, weddings, or business dinners, require a higher level of etiquette. These events often follow strict protocols, and understanding the rules can help you navigate them with confidence.

- **Understanding Place Settings and Utensils:** Formal place settings can be elaborate, with multiple utensils, glasses, and plates. Knowing how to navigate these settings is key to maintaining composure at the table.
- **The Basic Rule:** Start with the utensils on the outside and work your way in with each course. For example, the outermost fork is for the first course, often a salad, while the innermost fork is for the main course.
- **Specific Utensils:** Forks are typically placed on the left side of the plate, with the tines facing up. The number and size of the forks indicate their purpose—larger forks are for the main course, while smaller ones may be for salads or desserts. Knives are placed on the right side of the plate, with the cutting edge facing the plate. Spoons, used for soups or desserts, are also placed on the right. Glasses may include a water glass, a white wine glass, and a red wine glass, arranged diagonally above the knives.
- **Napkin Etiquette:** The napkin should be placed on your lap as soon as you sit down. If you need to leave the table during the meal, place your napkin on your chair. At the end of the meal, the napkin should be loosely folded and placed to the left of your plate. I've always found that these small acts, like correctly placing your napkin, signal to others that you are attentive and respectful, helping to set a positive tone for the entire meal.

Eating Different Types of Food Properly

Each type of food has its own etiquette, particularly in formal dining settings.

- **Bread:** Bread should be broken with your hands rather than cut with a knife. Break off a small piece at a time and butter it individually.
- **Soup:** When eating soup, dip the spoon away from you and sip from the side of the spoon rather than putting the whole spoon in your mouth. It's polite to avoid slurping.
- **Pasta:** Twirl a small amount of pasta on your fork using the side of your plate or a spoon for support. Avoid cutting pasta with a knife.
- **Fish:** Fish is typically eaten with a fish knife and fork. Use the knife to remove the skin and bones, and eat the flesh with the fork. If fish bones are present, gently remove them with your fingers and place them on the side of your plate.
- **Meat:** When cutting meat, use your knife and fork in tandem. Cut one piece at a time, and avoid cutting all your meat at once.

Mastering these techniques not only enhances your dining experience but also shows respect for the tradition and effort behind a formal meal. I remember the first time I attended a formal dinner where these rules were in full effect—it was a learning experience, but one that left a lasting impression on how I approach dining today.

Handling Toasts, Speeches, and Other Formalities

Toasts and speeches are common at formal dinners, and knowing how to handle them is important for maintaining decorum.

- **Making a Toast:** When making a toast, it's customary to stand, raise your glass, and make eye contact with the other guests. Keep the toast brief and focused on the occasion or the person being honored.
- **Responding to a Toast:** If you are the recipient of a toast, do

not drink to yourself. Instead, smile, acknowledge the toast, and raise your glass to the other guests.

- **Clinking Glasses:** In some cultures, it's customary to clink glasses when toasting. However, be gentle to avoid breaking the glass, and make eye contact with each person you clink with.
- **Speeches:** Speeches should be kept concise and relevant to the occasion. If you are asked to give a speech, prepare in advance and practice delivering it clearly and confidently. In my coaching sessions, I've often worked with clients on their public speaking skills, particularly for such formal occasions. It's not just about what you say, but how you say it —your tone, confidence, and ability to engage your audience are all crucial.

Casual Dining Etiquette

Manners for Informal Meals at Home or in Restaurants

Casual meals offer more flexibility, but some basic etiquette rules still apply to ensure a pleasant dining experience for everyone.

- **At Home:** When dining at someone's home, wait for the host to signal the start of the meal, usually by inviting everyone to begin eating. If you're helping yourself from shared dishes, take modest portions to ensure there's enough for everyone. Compliment the host on the meal, and offer to help with cleanup. In my own home, I've always appreciated guests who pitch in—these small acts of consideration create a warm, cooperative atmosphere.
- **In Restaurants:** When dining out, be respectful of the restaurant staff. This includes being polite when ordering, thanking the server when food is brought to the table, and addressing any issues with your meal calmly and respectfully. It's also important to keep your phone on silent and avoid loud conversations that might disturb other

diners. I've noticed that these small acts of courtesy often lead to better service and a more enjoyable dining experience for everyone involved.

The Etiquette of Potlucks, Picnics, and Barbecues

Potlucks, picnics, and barbecues are relaxed, social events where sharing food is central. However, these gatherings also have their own set of etiquette guidelines.

- **Potlucks:** When attending a potluck, bring a dish that is easy to share and complements the other dishes. It's considerate to bring serving utensils and to prepare your dish so it can be served without needing kitchen access. Always label your dish if it contains common allergens. I've hosted many potlucks, and the best ones are those where everyone contributes thoughtfully, making the event enjoyable and diverse in offerings.
- **Picnics:** For picnics, pack food that is easy to transport and eat outdoors, such as sandwiches, salads, or fruit. Bring enough to share, especially if it's a communal picnic. Be mindful of the environment by cleaning up all trash and leaving the picnic area as you found it.
- **Barbecues:** At a barbecue, it's polite to offer to bring something, whether it's food, drinks, or supplies. If you're the host, make sure there's enough seating and shade for your guests, and consider dietary restrictions when planning the menu. As a guest, be patient if the food takes time to cook and help out if needed. Some of the best conversations I've had were around the grill at a barbecue, where everyone pitched in and shared the experience.

Dining Out: Tipping, Complaints, and Special Requests

Dining out at a restaurant involves certain etiquette practices, especially when it comes to tipping, handling complaints, and making special requests.

- **Tipping:** In many cultures, tipping is a standard practice. In the United States, for example, it's customary to tip 15-20% of the total bill before tax. If you receive exceptional service, consider leaving a larger tip. In some countries, tipping is not expected, so it's important to be aware of local customs.
- **Handling Complaints:** If you encounter an issue with your meal, such as an incorrect order or undercooked food, address it politely with the server. Avoid raising your voice or being rude. Most restaurants will be happy to correct the mistake. If the problem is resolved satisfactorily, it's still appropriate to leave a tip.
- **Special Requests:** If you have dietary restrictions or preferences, it's best to inform the restaurant when making a reservation or before ordering. Be clear and polite about your needs, and thank the staff for accommodating them. If your request is complicated, consider giving the restaurant advance notice.

During my time as a coach, I've often emphasized the importance of these interactions. How you handle a small issue, like a dining complaint, can say a lot about your character and can set the tone for the rest of the meal.

Hosting and Attending Meals

The Art of Hosting with Grace and Hospitality

Hosting a meal requires careful planning and a focus on making your guests feel comfortable and welcome.

- **Planning the Menu:** Consider your guests' dietary restrictions and preferences when planning the menu. If you're unsure about someone's needs, it's polite to ask in advance. Aim for a balanced menu that includes options for different tastes and diets.

- **Setting the Table:** Even for casual meals, a thoughtfully set table enhances the dining experience. Ensure that all necessary utensils, glasses, and napkins are provided. For formal meals, follow the guidelines for place settings discussed earlier. I've always found that setting the table with care, even for a simple family dinner, can elevate the entire experience, making it feel special and intentional.
- **Welcoming Guests:** Greet each guest personally as they arrive, and offer them a drink or appetizer while waiting for everyone to arrive. If your guests are not familiar with each other, make introductions and encourage conversation.
- **Pacing the Meal:** As the host, it's your responsibility to pace the meal. Ensure that courses are served in a timely manner, and pay attention to your guests' needs. If someone's glass is empty or they need more bread, offer to replenish it.
- **Creating a Comfortable Atmosphere:** A successful meal is about more than just food; it's also about the atmosphere. Consider factors such as lighting, background music, and seating arrangements to create a comfortable and inviting environment. Encourage conversation and make sure everyone feels included.

In my experience, the best hosts are those who focus on the comfort and enjoyment of their guests, making the event as stress-free as possible. These are the gatherings that people remember fondly for years to come.

How to Be a Considerate Guest

As a guest, your role is to contribute positively to the event and show appreciation for the host's efforts.

- **RSVPing:** Always respond to an invitation promptly, whether you can attend or not. If you accept and later find that you cannot attend, inform the host as soon as possible.
- **Arriving on Time:** Punctuality is important, especially for formal meals. Arriving late can disrupt the meal's timing and

inconvenience the host. If you're running late due to unavoidable circumstances, inform the host and apologize upon arrival.

- **Bringing a Gift:** It's customary to bring a small gift for the host, such as a bottle of wine, flowers, or a homemade treat. The gift doesn't need to be extravagant but should reflect your appreciation.

- **Engaging with Others:** Participate actively in conversations and make an effort to engage with other guests. Be polite, listen attentively, and avoid dominating the conversation. If you're at a formal dinner, follow the lead of the host regarding conversation topics.

- **Thanking the Host:** Before leaving, thank the host personally for the meal and their hospitality. A follow-up thank-you note or message the next day is a thoughtful gesture that shows your appreciation.

Having hosted and attended many dinners over the years, I've seen firsthand how these small acts of consideration can make a big difference. As a guest, your behavior contributes to the overall success of the event, and your appreciation ensures that the host feels their efforts were worthwhile.

Handling Dietary Restrictions and Special Requests

Whether you're hosting or attending a meal, it's important to be mindful of dietary restrictions and special requests.

- **As a Host:** If you know that some of your guests have dietary restrictions, plan your menu accordingly. This might involve offering vegetarian, vegan, gluten-free, or allergen-free options. If you're unsure, it's polite to ask your guests in advance about their dietary needs. If accommodating a specific request is difficult, consider alternatives, such as preparing a separate dish or allowing the guest to bring their own food.

- **As a Guest:** If you have dietary restrictions, inform the host in advance. Be clear about your needs, but be flexible and understanding if the host cannot accommodate every request. If necessary, offer to bring a dish that you can eat and share with others.

- **Respecting Preferences:** Whether you're a host or guest, it's important to respect everyone's dietary preferences. Avoid making negative comments about someone's food choices or pressuring them to eat something they're uncomfortable with.

In my household, accommodating dietary preferences has become second nature. Whether for my neurodivergent children or guests with specific needs, I've found that being considerate in this way not only ensures everyone feels comfortable but also enhances the overall dining experience.

Practical Tips and Exercises

To help you refine your dining etiquette, here are some practical tips and exercises:

1. **Practice Place Settings:** Set a formal dining table with all the appropriate utensils, glasses, and napkins. Practice identifying which utensils to use for each course, and review the proper way to handle them.
2. **Cultural Dining Experience:** Choose a culture different from your own and research its dining customs. Then, visit a restaurant or prepare a meal from that culture, practicing the etiquette you've learned. Reflect on the experience and how it broadened your understanding of dining etiquette.
3. **Hosting a Dinner Party:** Host a small dinner party, paying attention to all aspects of etiquette—from setting the table to pacing the meal. After the event, ask your guests for feedback on their experience and reflect on what went well and what could be improved.
4. **Handling Dietary Requests:** Imagine you're hosting a

dinner with guests who have various dietary restrictions (e.g., vegan, gluten-free, kosher). Plan a menu that accommodates everyone's needs, and think through how you would handle any unexpected requests.

5. **Dining Out Role-Play**: With a friend, role-play a dining out scenario where you must address a complaint (e.g., incorrect order, undercooked food) politely and effectively. Practice tipping appropriately and handling any special requests with grace.

Conclusion: The Timeless Art of Dining Etiquette

The Importance of Respect and Consideration at the Table

Dining etiquette is not just about following rules—it's about fostering an atmosphere of respect, consideration, and enjoyment at the table. Whether in a formal setting, a casual meal, or when hosting or attending, practicing good manners ensures that everyone can enjoy the meal and the company.

Reflecting on my own experiences, I've seen how these practices contribute to a positive and memorable dining experience. The respect we show at the table often mirrors the respect we bring into our daily lives.

An Ongoing Journey of Learning and Refinement

Like all aspects of etiquette, dining etiquette is a skill that can be continually refined. Each meal presents an opportunity to practice and improve, whether it's mastering the use of utensils, understanding cultural nuances, or simply being a gracious host or guest.

For me, the journey of learning and refinement never ends. Each meal, each gathering, is an opportunity to connect, to grow, and to enhance our shared experiences.

Looking Ahead

As you continue through this guide, you'll explore further aspects of modern etiquette, including navigating complex social settings. These skills will not only enhance your dining experiences but also empower you to engage with others in a way that fosters respect, understanding, and genuine connection in every aspect of your life.

The art of dining is timeless, but it is also ever-evolving. By mastering these skills, you're not just learning to navigate meals—you're learning to navigate life with grace and respect.

TEN

SOCIAL MEDIA AND DIGITAL ETIQUETTE

IN THE DIGITAL AGE, where much of our communication and social interaction occurs online, understanding and practicing good etiquette in the virtual world is just as important as in the physical one. The digital realm can feel overwhelming at times, especially as our personal and professional lives increasingly overlap. Throughout my career as a relationship coach and my experiences navigating the online world, I've seen how the principles of respect, consideration, and professionalism apply just as powerfully in digital spaces as they do face-to-face. This chapter offers guidance on conducting yourself online in a way that's respectful, thoughtful, and conducive to building positive relationships.

Manners in the Digital Age

The Importance of Online Courtesy and Respect

Just as in face-to-face interactions, courtesy and respect are crucial in online communication. The relative anonymity of the internet can sometimes lead people to behave in ways they wouldn't in person, but it's important to remember that there are real people on the other side of the screen.

- **Think Before You Post:** Before posting anything online, consider its impact on others. Will it offend, hurt, or cause unnecessary conflict? Avoid posting when you're angry or upset, as emotions can cloud judgment and lead to regrettable actions. In my practice, I've often guided clients through the aftermath of a hasty online comment, reminding them that words, once shared, are hard to take back.
- **Be Mindful of Tone:** Tone can be easily misinterpreted online, especially in text-based communication where nuances like facial expressions and voice inflection are absent. Aim for a tone that is clear, polite, and considerate. Avoid sarcasm, as it often doesn't translate well online.
- **Respect Differences:** The internet is a global community where people of different cultures, beliefs, and backgrounds interact. Be respectful of differing opinions and avoid engaging in heated arguments. If you disagree with someone, do so politely and constructively. I've found that approaching online discussions with curiosity rather than confrontation leads to more meaningful exchanges.

Navigating Social Media with Professionalism and Care

Social media platforms are powerful tools for communication, networking, and self-expression. However, they also require careful management to maintain professionalism and respect for others.

- **Separate Personal and Professional Accounts:** If possible, maintain separate accounts for personal and professional use. This helps you manage your online presence more effectively and ensures that your professional image isn't compromised by personal content. Over the years, I've seen how blurred lines between personal and professional online personas can lead to misunderstandings and complications.
- **Think About Your Audience:** Before sharing anything on

social media, consider who will see it. Is it appropriate for all your connections? Could it be misinterpreted? Tailor your content to suit your audience and be mindful of the message you're sending.

- **Avoid Oversharing:** While social media encourages sharing, it's important to strike a balance. Avoid posting overly personal information, frequent complaints, or details that could harm your reputation or relationships. Keep in mind that once something is online, it's difficult to take back. I've learned from my own experience that maintaining some privacy online not only protects you but also preserves your personal and professional integrity.

Protecting Your Privacy and Respecting Others'

Privacy is a significant concern in the digital world, and protecting both your privacy and that of others is an important aspect of digital etiquette.

- **Manage Privacy Settings:** Regularly review and update your privacy settings on social media platforms to control who can see your content. Be selective about who you share personal information with and be cautious about accepting friend requests or connections from strangers.
- **Respect Others' Privacy:** Just as you value your privacy, respect the privacy of others. Avoid sharing personal information, photos, or details about someone else without their permission. This includes tagging people in posts— always ask before tagging someone in a photo or post, especially if it's in a personal or sensitive context.
- **Be Wary of Sharing Sensitive Content:** Think carefully before sharing content that could be considered sensitive or private, such as medical information, financial details, or personal grievances. Even in closed groups or private messages, there's a risk that this information could be shared

more widely than intended. In my coaching practice, I've often reminded clients that protecting one's privacy online is as important as safeguarding one's physical privacy.

Email and Text Etiquette

The Do's and Don'ts of Digital Communication

Email and text messaging are two of the most common forms of communication in the digital age. Understanding the do's and don'ts of these mediums is essential for effective and respectful communication.

- **Do Be Clear and Concise:** Whether sending an email or a text, keep your message clear and to the point. Avoid long-winded explanations or unnecessary details. If your message is complex, consider breaking it down into bullet points or numbered lists for clarity.
- **Do Use Proper Grammar and Punctuation:** Good grammar and punctuation are just as important in digital communication as they are in written correspondence. They help convey your message clearly and professionally. Avoid using all caps, which can be interpreted as shouting, and be mindful of spelling and grammar mistakes. I often tell clients that how we write is just as important as what we write—it reflects our attention to detail and our respect for the reader.
- **Don't Send Emails or Texts When Angry:** If you're upset, it's best to wait before responding. Take some time to cool off and consider your response carefully. Once you're calm, you can address the issue more rationally and respectfully.
- **Don't Overuse Emojis or Slang in Professional Communications:** While emojis and slang can add a casual tone to personal messages, they're often inappropriate in professional communications. Use them sparingly, and only if you're sure they'll be well-received by the recipient. In my

early career, I learned the hard way that what feels friendly and informal to one person can be seen as unprofessional by another.

Responding Promptly and Thoughtfully

Timely responses are a sign of respect and professionalism in digital communication.

- **Respond Promptly:** Aim to respond to emails and texts within 24 hours. If you need more time to formulate a response, send a quick acknowledgment to let the sender know you received their message and will get back to them soon.
- **Be Thoughtful in Your Responses:** Take the time to read the message carefully before responding. Address all points raised by the sender, and if you don't have an answer to a particular question, let them know you're looking into it. Avoid one-word responses, as they can come across as dismissive or uninterested. Thoughtful communication has always been a cornerstone of my work, and I've seen how it can strengthen relationships and build trust.

Handling Misunderstandings and Conflicts Online

Misunderstandings and conflicts can easily arise in digital communication due to the lack of non-verbal cues. Knowing how to handle these situations is key to maintaining positive relationships.

- **Clarify Before Reacting:** If you receive a message that seems harsh or unclear, seek clarification before reacting. A simple question like, "Could you clarify what you meant by this?" can prevent misunderstandings and allow for a more measured response.
- **Apologize When Necessary:** If you realize that you've misunderstood or miscommunicated something, apologize

promptly and sincerely. Acknowledge the mistake and offer a solution or clarification to move forward.

- **Avoid Public Disputes:** If a conflict arises, handle it privately rather than airing grievances publicly on social media or in group emails. Public disputes can escalate quickly and damage relationships, so it's best to address issues one-on-one. Early in my career, I witnessed how public online disputes can lead to long-lasting damage, underscoring the importance of private, respectful communication.

Maintaining a Positive Online Presence

Building and Managing Your Personal Brand

Your online presence contributes significantly to your personal brand, especially in professional contexts. It's important to manage this presence carefully to reflect your values, skills, and professionalism.

- **Consistency is Key:** Ensure that your online profiles, including LinkedIn, Twitter, and personal websites, present a consistent and professional image. This includes using the same professional photo across platforms, aligning your bio and messaging, and being mindful of the content you share. Over the years, I've worked with clients to help them craft personal brands that are not only professional but also authentically reflect who they are.
- **Share Thoughtfully:** The content you share online contributes to your personal brand. Share articles, posts, and updates that reflect your interests, expertise, and values. Avoid sharing content that could be controversial or misaligned with your professional goals.
- **Engage Positively:** Engage with others online in a positive and constructive manner. This includes commenting on posts, sharing insights, and participating in discussions in a way that adds value to the conversation.

Engaging with Others Online: Likes, Comments, and Shares

Interacting with others on social media through likes, comments, and shares is a key aspect of building relationships online. However, these actions should be thoughtful and considerate.

- **Like with Intention:** Liking a post is a simple way to show support, but it's important to do so with intention. Avoid liking content that could be considered inappropriate, offensive, or irrelevant to your brand.
- **Comment Respectfully:** When commenting on posts, be respectful and constructive. Avoid making negative or critical remarks, especially in public forums. If you disagree with something, express your opinion politely and provide reasons for your perspective.
- **Share Responsibly:** Sharing content is a powerful way to amplify messages, but be mindful of what you're endorsing. Verify the accuracy of the content before sharing it, and ensure it aligns with your values and brand.

The Etiquette of Digital Networking and Collaborations

Digital networking and collaborations are increasingly common, especially in professional settings. Following proper etiquette can help you build strong and fruitful relationships online.

- **Be Professional in Your Outreach:** When reaching out to someone for networking or collaboration purposes, be clear about your intentions and respectful of their time. A concise and well-written message that outlines who you are, why you're reaching out, and how you believe the collaboration could be mutually beneficial is most effective.
- **Follow Up Appropriately:** If you don't receive a response to your initial outreach, it's appropriate to send a polite follow-up message after a reasonable amount of time, typically one to two weeks. Avoid being overly persistent, as this can come across as pushy. Patience and respect have always been key in

my professional relationships, and they've helped me build lasting connections.

- **Show Appreciation:** When someone agrees to collaborate or network with you, express your gratitude. After a successful collaboration or meeting, send a thank-you email or message to acknowledge their time and effort.

Practical Tips and Exercises

To help you refine your social media and digital etiquette, here are some practical tips and exercises:

1. **Review Your Social Media Profiles:** Take some time to review all your social media profiles. Ensure that your profile pictures, bios, and content are consistent and reflect the image you want to project. Remove any posts or comments that might be considered unprofessional or outdated.

2. **Practice Thoughtful Posting:** Before you post something online, pause and consider its impact. Ask yourself if it's respectful, necessary, and aligned with your values. Make a habit of posting content that adds value to your audience.

3. **Email and Text Etiquette Drill:** Choose a recent email or text conversation and analyze it for tone, clarity, and professionalism. Consider how you could improve your communication in future interactions, and practice writing clear, concise, and respectful messages.

4. **Conflict Resolution Role-Play:** With a friend or colleague, role-play a scenario where a misunderstanding has occurred in an email or online conversation. Practice responding in a way that seeks clarification, defuses tension, and resolves the issue constructively.

5. **Digital Networking Practice:** Identify someone you'd like to connect with professionally online. Craft a thoughtful and respectful message to introduce yourself and explain why you'd like to connect. Practice following up and expressing gratitude after the interaction.

Conclusion: Navigating the Digital World with Grace

The Role of Etiquette in a Connected World

As our lives become increasingly intertwined with the digital world, the principles of etiquette remain as important as ever. Respect, consideration, and professionalism should guide all online interactions, ensuring that we contribute positively to the digital spaces we inhabit.

Reflecting on my own experiences, I've seen firsthand how online interactions can either strengthen relationships or create unnecessary conflicts. The way we communicate online can have lasting impacts, both positive and negative, on our personal and professional lives.

An Ongoing Commitment to Courtesy and Respect

Digital etiquette is an ongoing commitment that requires mindfulness and adaptability. By continually refining your online behavior, you can build stronger relationships, maintain a positive online presence, and navigate the complexities of the digital world with grace and confidence.

Throughout my career, I've learned that the principles of courtesy and respect are timeless, and they apply equally in digital interactions as they do in face-to-face encounters. These principles not only help us navigate the digital world but also contribute to a more respectful and connected global community.

Looking Ahead

As you continue through this guide, you'll explore further aspects of modern etiquette. These skills will not only enhance your digital interactions but also empower you to engage with others in a way that fosters respect, understanding, and genuine connection in every aspect of your life.

The digital world offers endless opportunities for connection, learning, and growth. By mastering the etiquette that governs these spaces, you're not just building a positive online presence—you're contributing to a more respectful and compassionate digital community.

ELEVEN

TRAVEL ETIQUETTE

TRAVELING OFFERS a unique opportunity to experience new cultures, meet new people, and explore unfamiliar places. However, it also comes with the responsibility of conducting oneself with courtesy and respect, both towards fellow travelers and the people and places you encounter on your journey. Throughout my five years living overseas and traveling to over 20 countries, I've learned that travel etiquette is not just about following rules—it's about embracing the spirit of respect and connection that makes every journey richer and more rewarding. This chapter provides a comprehensive guide to travel etiquette, ensuring that your adventures are enjoyable for everyone involved.

Traveling with Courtesy

Manners for Air, Rail, and Road Travel

Traveling in close quarters with others requires a heightened awareness of your behavior. Whether you're on a plane, train, bus, or car, courtesy and consideration can make the journey more pleasant for everyone.

- **Air Travel:**
- **Boarding and Disembarking:** Board the plane in an orderly fashion, respecting others' turn and the boarding groups. When disembarking, wait for your row to be called and avoid pushing or rushing ahead. During one of my flights to Southeast Asia, I witnessed how a calm and patient boarding process set the tone for a peaceful journey, even on a long-haul flight.
- **Overhead Bins:** Use the overhead bins sparingly, placing only your larger carry-on items there and keeping smaller items under the seat in front of you. If you're traveling with a smaller item that doesn't need to go in the overhead bin, offer to place it under your seat to save space for others.
- **Seat Etiquette:** Recline your seat carefully and slowly, checking to ensure the person behind you isn't inconvenienced. Keep your area tidy and avoid using the tray table as a rest for your head or feet. If you need to get up, do so gently to avoid disturbing your seatmates.
- **Noise Control:** Keep noise to a minimum by using headphones for audio devices and speaking quietly. Avoid loud conversations or phone calls, and be mindful of your volume, especially on overnight flights.
- **Rail Travel:**
- **Respecting Space:** On trains, where seating can be more communal, be mindful of your space. Keep your belongings within your area and avoid spreading out to take up more than your share of the seat.
- **Quiet Zones:** Many trains have designated quiet zones where loud conversations, phone calls, and noisy activities are discouraged. Respect these zones by keeping noise to a minimum. During a trip across Europe, I found the quiet zones to be a haven for rest and reflection, a stark contrast to the hustle of the train stations.
- **Exiting the Train:** As with air travel, allow those closest to the exit to leave first. Don't push or rush to disembark, and be patient as others collect their belongings.

- **Road Travel:**
- **Car Etiquette:** When traveling by car with others, be considerate of your fellow passengers. This includes keeping the car clean, sharing control of the music or climate settings, and respecting personal space. If you're the driver, prioritize safety and comfort for all passengers.
- **Public Buses and Coaches:** When using public transportation, offer your seat to those who need it more, such as the elderly, pregnant women, or people with disabilities. Keep conversations at a low volume and avoid eating strong-smelling foods.

Navigating Airports and Stations with Grace

Airports, train stations, and bus terminals are often bustling with activity, and navigating these spaces with grace is essential for a smooth travel experience.

- **Security Checks:** Be prepared for security checks by having your documents and items ready for inspection. Follow instructions promptly and politely, and be patient with security personnel, as they are doing their job to ensure everyone's safety. I remember my first time going through security in a foreign country—I was nervous and uncertain, but a kind smile from a fellow traveler reminded me that patience is universal.
- **Queueing:** Respect the queue system at check-in, security, boarding, and ticket counters. Avoid cutting in line or saving spots for others, as this can cause frustration and delays for everyone else.
- **Personal Space:** In crowded areas, such as baggage claim or boarding gates, be mindful of personal space. Avoid crowding others and keep a comfortable distance whenever possible.
- **Assisting Others:** If you see someone struggling with luggage, directions, or mobility, offer assistance if you're able

to do so. A small act of kindness can significantly improve someone's travel experience.

The Etiquette of Sharing Public Spaces

Public spaces, such as airports, lounges, and transportation hubs, are shared environments where everyone's comfort is important. Practicing good etiquette in these spaces ensures a pleasant atmosphere for all.

- **Lounge Etiquette:** If you have access to an airport or train lounge, remember that it's a shared space. Keep noise to a minimum, avoid hogging seats or power outlets, and clean up after yourself. If you're using a laptop or device, keep it on silent or use headphones.
- **Restroom Courtesy:** Public restrooms should be left as clean as you found them. Dispose of trash properly, flush after use, and report any issues to staff rather than leaving a mess for the next person.
- **Respecting Quiet Areas:** Many public spaces have designated quiet areas for those who need rest or want to work undisturbed. Respect these zones by keeping noise to a minimum and avoiding phone calls or loud conversations.

Hotel and Accommodation Etiquette

Respecting Hotel Staff and Fellow Guests

Hotels and other accommodations are places where many people come together, often from different backgrounds and cultures. Respecting both the staff and other guests is key to maintaining a pleasant environment.

- **Check-In and Check-Out:** Arrive on time for check-in and check-out, and if you're running late, inform the hotel to avoid inconveniencing others. Be patient with front desk staff, especially during busy periods, and express any concerns calmly and respectfully. During my time living abroad, I often found that a polite check-in could set the tone for the entire stay, even in the most bustling hotels.

- **Tipping Guidelines:** In many places, it's customary to tip hotel staff, such as bellhops, housekeeping, and room service. A standard tip is typically a few dollars per service, though this can vary depending on the country and the level of service. If you're unsure, ask the front desk for guidance.

- **Noise Levels:** Be mindful of noise in your room, especially in the evening or early morning. Keep the volume of the TV or music low, avoid loud conversations, and close doors gently to minimize disturbance to other guests.

- **Housekeeping Etiquette:** Leave your room in reasonable order for housekeeping staff. This includes placing used towels in one area, disposing of trash in bins, and keeping personal items organized. If you don't need daily housekeeping, consider using the "Do Not Disturb" sign to give staff a break.

Tipping Guidelines and Special Requests

Understanding tipping practices and making special requests with courtesy can enhance your experience and show respect for the staff's hard work.

- **Tipping Standards:** Tipping practices vary by country, but in many places, it's customary to tip housekeeping, bellhops, and room service. In the U.S., for example, tipping $2-5 per night for housekeeping is standard, while in Europe, tipping might be less common. Always check local customs and tip accordingly.

- **Making Special Requests:** If you have special requests, such as extra towels, late check-out, or specific room preferences, ask politely and well in advance. Understand that not all requests can be accommodated, and be gracious if the staff is unable to fulfill them.

- **Expressing Gratitude:** A simple thank you goes a long way in showing appreciation for the services provided by hotel staff. Whether it's a note left for housekeeping or a verbal thank you to the front desk, expressing gratitude can enhance your stay and foster positive relationships.

The Do's and Don'ts of Using Shared Amenities

Shared amenities, such as pools, gyms, and lounges, are common in hotels and resorts. Using these spaces with respect ensures that all guests can enjoy them.

- **Pool and Gym Etiquette:** Follow posted rules for pool and gym use, such as showering before entering the pool, wiping down equipment after use, and wearing appropriate attire. Avoid monopolizing equipment or lounge chairs, and respect the space of others.
- **Breakfast Buffets:** At hotel breakfast buffets, be mindful of other guests. Use tongs and utensils provided, take only what you need, and avoid lingering at the buffet. If you spill or drop something, notify the staff so they can address it quickly. One morning in a bustling Parisian hotel, I learned how a simple smile and "merci" could turn a chaotic breakfast into a more pleasant experience.
- **Business Centers and Lounges:** When using business centers or lounges, keep your time there to a reasonable limit, especially if others are waiting. If you're using shared computers or printers, log out of personal accounts and dispose of sensitive documents properly.

Cultural Sensitivity in Travel

Understanding and Respecting Local Customs

Traveling to a new country or region often means encountering different cultural practices and customs. Understanding and respecting these customs is a crucial part of travel etiquette.

- **Research Before You Go:** Before traveling, take the time to research the customs and traditions of your destination. This includes understanding social norms, religious practices, and local laws. For example, in some cultures, it's customary to remove your shoes before entering someone's home, while in others, certain gestures or clothing might be considered inappropriate.
- **Respecting Religious Sites:** When visiting religious sites, such as temples, churches, or mosques, dress modestly and follow any rules regarding behavior, photography, or silence. Always be respectful of worshippers and avoid disrupting religious ceremonies or services.
- **Tipping and Bartering:** Tipping and bartering practices can vary widely between cultures. In some places, tipping is expected and appreciated, while in others, it might be seen as inappropriate. Similarly, bartering may be a common practice in markets in some regions but not in others. Understanding these practices helps you engage respectfully with local vendors and service providers.

The Importance of Learning Basic Phrases and Gestures

Learning a few basic phrases and gestures in the local language shows respect and can greatly enhance your travel experience.

- **Basic Phrases:** Learn basic phrases such as "hello," "thank you," "please," and "excuse me" in the local language. These small efforts can go a long way in showing respect for the local culture and making interactions smoother.
- **Non-Verbal Communication:** Be aware of local non-verbal communication cues, such as gestures, eye contact, and personal space. For example, in some cultures, a handshake is customary, while in others, a bow or nod is more appropriate. Understanding these cues can help you navigate social interactions with greater ease.

- **Using Translation Tools:** If you're traveling to a place where you don't speak the language, consider using translation apps or carrying a phrasebook. These tools can help you communicate more effectively and show that you're making an effort to engage with the local culture.

How to Be a Considerate and Responsible Tourist

Being a responsible tourist involves more than just following the rules—it's about contributing positively to the places you visit and leaving them better than you found them.

- **Respect the Environment:** Whether you're exploring a natural park, beach, or urban area, always respect the environment. Dispose of trash properly, avoid disturbing wildlife, and follow any guidelines for protecting natural or cultural heritage sites.
- **Support Local Economies:** Whenever possible, support local businesses by eating at local restaurants, staying in locally-owned accommodations, and purchasing souvenirs from local artisans. This not only enhances your experience but also contributes to the local economy. During my travels through small villages in Asia, I found that engaging with local artisans not only enriched my understanding of their culture but also provided them with meaningful support.
- **Be Mindful of Photography:** Always ask for permission before taking photos of people, especially in cultures where this might be seen as intrusive or disrespectful. Be mindful of signs prohibiting photography in certain areas, such as religious sites or private properties.
- **Travel Lightly:** Consider the environmental impact of your travel choices. Use public transportation, reduce plastic waste, and be conscious of your energy and water usage in hotels. Responsible travel is about minimizing your footprint and respecting the resources of the places you visit.

Practical Tips and Exercises

To help you refine your travel etiquette, here are some practical tips and exercises:

1. **Research Exercise:** Before your next trip, research the cultural customs, tipping practices, and social norms of your destination. Make a list of key points to remember, such as dress codes for religious sites, local greetings, and appropriate tipping amounts.

2. **Practice Basic Phrases:** Learn and practice basic phrases in the language of the country you're visiting. Use language apps, flashcards, or online resources to build your vocabulary, and challenge yourself to use these phrases during your trip.

3. **Packing Light Challenge:** Challenge yourself to pack only the essentials for your next trip. Focus on minimizing waste, such as bringing a reusable water bottle and tote bag, and consider the environmental impact of the items you bring.

4. **Hotel Etiquette Role-Play:** With a friend or family member, role-play different hotel scenarios, such as making a special request, tipping staff, or addressing a noisy neighbor. Practice handling these situations politely and effectively.

5. **Cultural Sensitivity Reflection:** Reflect on a past travel experience where you encountered a cultural difference. Consider how you handled the situation and what you learned. Think about how you can apply this experience to future travels.

Conclusion: The Joy of Respectful Travel

The Role of Etiquette in Enhancing Travel Experiences

Traveling with courtesy, cultural sensitivity, and respect for others not only enriches your own experiences but also contributes to the well-being of the people and places you visit. By practicing good travel etiquette, you can ensure that your journeys are enjoyable, meaningful, and memorable.

An Ongoing Journey of Learning and Exploration

Travel etiquette is an ongoing learning process, as every destination brings new customs, challenges, and opportunities for growth. By remaining open-minded and respectful, you can navigate the world with grace and leave a positive impact wherever you go.

Looking Ahead

As you continue through this guide, the final chapter will explore special occasion etiquette, offering guidance on navigating celebrations and other important events with poise and consideration. These skills, combined with those you've learned in this chapter, will empower you to engage with others in a way that fosters respect, understanding, and genuine connection.

THROUGHOUT MY YEARS OF TRAVEL, the lessons I've learned about respect, curiosity, and connection have stayed with me, enriching not only my journeys but also my understanding of the world. May your travels be filled with discovery, joy, and the simple grace of good etiquette.

TWELVE

SPECIAL OCCASION ETIQUETTE

SPECIAL OCCASIONS, whether joyful celebrations or solemn events, offer opportunities to connect with others and show our respect and appreciation. These moments often come with unique expectations and traditions, making it important to approach them with sensitivity, thoughtfulness, and an understanding of the appropriate etiquette. Drawing from my experiences of attending countless weddings, funerals, and family gatherings, I've come to appreciate how vital these practices are in ensuring that these events are meaningful and respectful. This final chapter covers the nuances of etiquette for holidays, funerals, and significant life milestones, helping you navigate these occasions with grace and consideration.

Holiday and Festive Etiquette

Hosting and Attending Holiday Gatherings

Holidays are times for gathering with loved ones, but they can also bring stress and challenges, especially when hosting or attending events.

- **Hosting:** As a host, your role is to create a welcoming and festive atmosphere for your guests. Plan ahead to ensure that your home is prepared, including decorating, preparing food, and considering any dietary restrictions your guests may have. Send out invitations well in advance, and if your event is a potluck, clearly communicate what each guest should bring. During the event, be attentive to your guests' needs, and strive to include everyone in conversations and activities. I've hosted many holiday gatherings, and I've found that the most successful ones are those where the host anticipates the needs of their guests, making everyone feel at home.

- **Attending:** When attending a holiday gathering, it's important to RSVP promptly and bring a small gift for the host, such as a bottle of wine, a box of chocolates, or a festive decoration. Arrive on time, and offer to help the host with any last-minute preparations. Be mindful of the event's atmosphere—whether it's a lively celebration or a more subdued gathering—and adjust your behavior accordingly. I still recall the warmth I felt when a guest arrived at one of my holiday dinners with a homemade pie, not only as a gesture of appreciation but also as a meaningful contribution to the gathering.

Gift-Giving Etiquette for Holidays and Special Occasions

Gift-giving is a central part of many holidays and special occasions, but it can also be a source of anxiety. Understanding the expectations and cultural norms around gift-giving can help alleviate some of this pressure.

- **Choosing the Right Gift:** When selecting a gift, consider the recipient's interests, preferences, and any cultural or religious customs that might influence your choice. Thoughtfulness is key—a personalized or meaningful gift is often more appreciated than something expensive or extravagant. I remember a time when a friend gave me a book that resonated deeply with my interests—it was a simple gift, but its impact was profound because it reflected how well she knew me.

- **Presenting Gifts:** When giving a gift, present it with sincerity and without expecting anything in return. In some cultures, it's customary to refuse a gift once or twice before accepting it, so be patient and gracious during this exchange. If you receive a gift, express your gratitude immediately, either verbally or with a thank-you note.
- **Regifting:** Regifting is generally considered acceptable as long as the gift is appropriate for the new recipient and hasn't been used. However, be careful to avoid regifting in a way that could offend the original giver or the new recipient.

Navigating Family Dynamics During Festive Seasons

The holiday season can sometimes bring family tensions to the surface. Navigating these dynamics with tact and understanding is crucial for maintaining harmony.

- **Respecting Traditions:** Every family has its own traditions and expectations for holiday celebrations. Even if these differ from your own preferences, make an effort to participate and respect the customs that are important to your family or your partner's family. Over the years, I've learned to appreciate the variety of traditions in my extended family, from elaborate Christmas Eve dinners to quiet New Year's Day reflections, each offering a unique way to connect and celebrate.
- **Managing Conflicts:** If tensions arise, try to remain calm and avoid escalating the situation. Choose your battles wisely, and remember that the holidays are a time for togetherness and joy. If necessary, step away from a heated discussion and return when emotions have cooled.
- **Balancing Obligations:** The holiday season often involves multiple gatherings with different branches of the family.

Plan your schedule carefully to ensure that you can attend key events without overextending yourself. Communicate openly with your family about your plans, and be respectful of others' time and commitments.

Funerals and Mourning Etiquette

Appropriate Behavior and Attire at Funerals

Funerals are solemn occasions that require sensitivity, respect, and an understanding of the cultural or religious practices involved.

- **Attire:** Traditional funeral attire is typically conservative, often involving dark colors like black, navy, or gray. Avoid bright colors or flashy accessories, and choose clothing that is modest and respectful. If the family has requested a specific dress code or attire that reflects the deceased's personality, such as wearing their favorite color, honor this request. At a funeral I attended for a close friend's father, the family asked everyone to wear bright colors to celebrate his life—honoring this request brought comfort and unity during a difficult time.
- **Behavior:** At a funeral, your behavior should reflect the solemnity of the occasion. Arrive on time, and if you must arrive late, enter quietly and take a seat at the back. Follow the lead of the officiant and the family regarding when to stand, sit, or participate in rituals. If you're unsure of what to do, it's perfectly acceptable to observe quietly and respectfully.

Offering Condolences and Support

Expressing sympathy and offering support to those who are grieving is a vital part of mourning etiquette.

- **Offering Condolences:** When offering condolences, be sincere and compassionate. Simple phrases like "I'm so sorry for your loss" or "You and your family are in my thoughts" can be comforting. Avoid saying anything that might minimize the person's grief, such as "They're in a better place" or "It was meant to be." If you're close to the family, consider sending a sympathy card, flowers, or making a charitable donation in the deceased's name. I've found that the most meaningful condolences often come from simple, heartfelt words that acknowledge the depth of the loss without trying to fix it.

- **Providing Support:** Grieving families often appreciate practical support, such as helping with meals, childcare, or errands. Offer your assistance without being intrusive, and be sensitive to their need for privacy and time alone.

Handling Cultural Differences in Mourning Practices

Different cultures have varying practices and traditions for mourning and funerals. Understanding and respecting these differences is essential.

- **Research and Awareness:** If you're attending a funeral that involves customs or rituals unfamiliar to you, take the time to research and understand what to expect. This might include specific prayers, rituals, or mourning periods. Being informed shows respect for the family's traditions.
- **Participation:** If you're invited to participate in a ritual or custom, do so with respect and sincerity. If you're uncomfortable or unsure about participating, it's acceptable to decline politely and observe from the sidelines. During a trip to India, I attended a Hindu funeral ceremony that was vastly different from the Western practices I was familiar with. Observing and respecting the rituals, even as an outsider, allowed me to support my friend in a deeply meaningful way.

Etiquette for Birthdays, Anniversaries, and Graduations

Life's milestones—such as birthdays, anniversaries, and graduations—are important occasions that call for celebration and recognition.

- **Birthday Celebrations:** Whether you're hosting or attending a birthday party, it's important to honor the person whose day it is. As a guest, bring a thoughtful gift and arrive on time. If you're the host, plan the event according to the birthday person's preferences, whether they prefer a large gathering or a more intimate celebration. One of my favorite memories is of a surprise birthday party I planned for a dear friend, where every detail reflected her unique personality and interests.

- **Anniversaries:** Anniversaries, particularly those marking significant milestones, are a time to celebrate a couple's journey together. If you're invited to an anniversary celebration, bring a gift that honors the couple's relationship, such as a personalized item or something that reflects their shared interests. If you're planning the event, consider including elements that highlight the couple's memories and achievements.

- **Graduations:** Graduations are a time to celebrate academic achievements and the transition to a new phase of life. When attending a graduation, dress appropriately for the occasion, and bring a congratulatory card or gift. If you're the graduate, express gratitude to those who supported you along the way, whether through a speech, thank-you notes, or personal acknowledgments.

Hosting and Attending Milestone Events with Respect

Hosting or attending milestone events requires a balance of celebration and respect for the significance of the occasion.

- **Hosting:** When hosting a milestone event, plan carefully to ensure that the celebration is meaningful and enjoyable for the honoree. This might include organizing speeches, toasts, or presentations that highlight their achievements. Be attentive to the needs of your guests, and ensure that everyone feels included in the celebration.
- **Attending:** As a guest at a milestone event, your role is to honor the occasion and support the honoree. Arrive on time, participate in any planned activities, and offer your congratulations or well-wishes. If speeches or toasts are given, listen attentively and join in any group acknowledgments, such as raising a glass for a toast.

The Importance of Acknowledging Others' Achievements

Acknowledging the achievements and milestones of others is a key aspect of social etiquette, fostering goodwill and strengthening relationships.

- **Congratulatory Messages:** Whether in person, through a card, or via social media, taking the time to acknowledge someone's achievements shows that you care about their success. Be sincere in your congratulations, and avoid making comparisons or shifting the focus to yourself.
- **Participating in Celebrations:** Even if you're not close to the honoree, participating in their celebrations is a way to show support and respect. This might include attending their event, contributing to a group gift, or simply sending a message of congratulations.
- **Respecting Privacy:** Some people prefer to keep their milestones private or celebrate in a low-key manner. Respect their wishes, and avoid pressuring them to celebrate in a way that makes them uncomfortable.

Practical Tips and Exercises

To help you refine your special occasion etiquette, here are some practical tips and exercises:

1. **Practice Writing Condolence Messages:** Write a few sample condolence messages for different scenarios, such as the loss of a loved one, a pet, or a colleague. Focus on being sincere, compassionate, and supportive.
2. **Plan a Milestone Celebration:** Imagine you're hosting a milestone event, such as a 50th wedding anniversary or a graduation party. Plan the details, including invitations, venue, menu, and activities, while keeping the honoree's preferences and the significance of the occasion in mind.
3. **Gift-Giving Exercise:** Make a list of upcoming special occasions and brainstorm thoughtful gift ideas for each. Consider the recipient's interests, cultural background, and any specific customs that might influence your choice.
4. **Cultural Awareness Reflection:** Reflect on a special occasion you've attended that involved different cultural or religious practices. Consider what you learned from the experience and how you can apply this knowledge to future events.
5. **Role-Play Holiday Gatherings:** With a friend or family member, role-play scenarios that might arise during holiday gatherings, such as managing a family conflict or navigating a sensitive conversation. Practice responding with tact and diplomacy.

Conclusion: Navigating Life's Special Moments with Grace

Celebrating with Respect and Consideration

Special occasions, whether joyful or solemn, provide opportunities to connect with others, honor traditions, and celebrate life's milestones. By approaching these moments with respect, thoughtfulness, and understanding, you can help ensure that they are meaningful and memorable for everyone involved.

Continuing the Journey of Etiquette

As you conclude this guide, remember that etiquette is not a set of rigid rules but a way of showing care and respect for others in every interaction. Whether at a festive gathering, a solemn funeral, or a celebratory milestone, the principles of good etiquette guide us toward stronger, more harmonious relationships.

Looking Forward

While this chapter marks the end of your exploration of modern etiquette, the journey of learning and applying these principles continues. As you encounter new situations and challenges, remember to draw on the skills and insights you've gained. By doing so, you will continue to navigate the complexities of social life with grace, confidence, and an enduring commitment to respect and understanding.

THROUGHOUT THE YEARS, from the joyful milestones to the solemn farewells, the practice of good etiquette has been a constant guide, helping me to navigate these moments with care and grace. May the lessons of this guide empower you to do the same, bringing a spirit of respect and kindness to every special occasion you encounter.

THIRTEEN

CONCLUSION

The Ongoing Importance of Etiquette

IN A WORLD that is constantly evolving, where technology often shapes our interactions and social norms are in flux, the value of good manners remains timeless. Etiquette is not just about following rules; it's about fostering respect, understanding, and connection in our daily lives. It serves as the foundation for successful relationships, whether personal or professional, and it provides the framework for navigating the complexities of modern life with grace and confidence.

As someone who has spent decades working as a relationship coach, I have witnessed firsthand the profound impact that good manners—or the lack thereof—can have on relationships. I've seen how a thoughtful gesture can mend a rift, how a simple act of courtesy can turn a potential conflict into a cooperative conversation, and how showing respect for others can open doors to opportunities and deeper connections. These experiences have reinforced my belief that, no matter how much the world changes, the core principles of etiquette will always matter.

To continue improving your social skills, I encourage you to stay curious and open-minded. Etiquette is a lifelong learning process, and every interaction is an opportunity to refine your approach. Whether you're attending a formal event, navigating the complexities of social media, or simply sharing a meal with friends, take a moment to consider how your actions and words can contribute to a more positive and harmonious environment.

Leading by example is one of the most powerful ways to influence others. When you consistently practice good manners, you set a standard for those around you, inspiring them to do the same. Your behavior becomes a model for others, showing that kindness, respect, and consideration are not just niceties, but essential elements of a successful and fulfilling life.

AFTERWORD

Embracing etiquette as a tool for success and harmony doesn't mean adhering to rigid rules or sacrificing your authenticity. Rather, it's about integrating the principles of respect, empathy, and thoughtfulness into your daily interactions. These principles are the bedrock of positive relationships and are key to navigating life's challenges with dignity and grace.

Throughout my career, I've observed that the most successful and fulfilled individuals are those who prioritize their relationships and treat others with kindness and respect. They understand that good manners are not just about making a good impression, but about building lasting connections based on mutual understanding and trust.

As you move forward, I encourage you to practice what you've learned in this book. Whether you're traveling the world, attending a special occasion, or simply engaging with others online, remember that your actions have the power to shape your relationships and your environment. By committing to the principles of modern etiquette, you can create a positive impact in your own life and in the lives of those around you.

Thank you for joining me on this journey through the world of etiquette. I hope that the insights and guidance shared here will serve you well as you navigate the ever-changing landscape of social interactions. Remember, the true essence of etiquette lies in the intention behind your actions—an intention to foster respect, understanding, and harmony in all that you do.

ABOUT THE AUTHOR

Rebecca Ferguson is a seasoned relationship coach with over 20 years of experience helping individuals and couples navigate the complexities of human connections. Rebecca has dedicated her career to guiding people toward more fulfilling relationships, both in their personal lives and within the broader social fabric. Her deep understanding of human behavior, combined with her compassionate approach, has made her a sought-after coach and speaker.

Throughout her career, Rebecca has worked with a diverse range of clients, from those facing significant life transitions to those simply seeking to enhance their interpersonal skills. Her expertise extends beyond traditional relationship advice, encompassing a holistic approach that includes personal growth, emotional intelligence, and the practical application of modern etiquette.

Having lived overseas for five years and traveled to over 20 countries, Rebecca brings a global perspective to her work. She understands the importance of cultural sensitivity and inclusivity in today's interconnected world, and she is passionate about helping others navigate these dynamics with grace and respect.

In addition to her coaching practice, Rebecca is a dedicated advocate for inclusive etiquette, believing that respect and understanding are the cornerstones of meaningful relationships. Her insights have empowered countless individuals to approach social interactions with confidence, empathy, and a commitment to fostering genuine connections.

Rebecca lives in Melbourne, where she continues to inspire and support others through her coaching, writing, and workshops. When she's not working, she enjoys exploring new cultures, spending time with her family, and embracing the vibrant community around her.

I VALUE YOUR FEEDBACK

Thank you for choosing *The Ultimate Guide to Modern Etiquette*. Your journey through the art of social graces, professional decorum, and cultural etiquette is just beginning, and we hope this book has provided you with valuable insights and practical guidance.

If you found *The Ultimate Guide to Modern Etiquette* helpful, I kindly ask you to consider leaving a review. Your feedback not only helps me, the author, continue to refine my work but also assists other readers in deciding whether this book will meet their needs. Whether you share your thoughts on how this guide has enhanced your social skills, or offer suggestions for future editions, your voice matters.

Leaving a review is a wonderful way to contribute to the community of readers who, like you, are committed to living graciously and navigating social interactions with confidence and respect. Thank you for helping me spread the word about the importance of modern etiquette in our lives.

You might also consider buying my other book, *The Soulmate Equation: The Ultimate Formula for Finding, Dating and Keeping a Quality Man*.

www.ingramcontent.com/pod-product-compliance
Lightning Source LLC
Chambersburg PA
CBHW032113280326
41933CB00009B/816